SOUPiNG

Alison Velázquez

To my family, who have beer

Publisher: Mike Sanders
Associate Publisher: Billy Fields
Senior Acquisitions Editor: Brook Farling
Development Editor: Ann Barton
Senior Jacket Creative: Nicola Powling
Book Designer: XAB Design
Photographer: Brian Wetzstein
Food Stylist: Mollie Hayward
Prepress Technician: Brian Massey
Proofreader: Laura Caddell
Indexer: Heather McNeill

Editor: Caroline Curtis
Project editor: Kathryn Meeker
Senior art editor: Glenda Fisher
Jacket designer: Harriet Yeomans, Amy Keast
Senior pre-production producer: Rebecca Fallowfield
Senior producer: Stephanie McConnell
Creative technical support: Sonia Charbonnier
Managing editor: Stephanie Farrow
Managing art editor: Christine Keilty

First British Edition, 2016
Published in Great Britain by Dorling Kindersley Limited
80 Strand, London WC2R 0RL

Copyright © 2016 Dorling Kindersley Limited
A Penguin Random House Company
10 9 8 7 6 5 4 3 2 1
001-290242-January2016

A CIP catalogue record for this book is available from the British Library.

ISBN: 978-0-2412-4555-2

Printed and bound in Slovakia

All images © Dorling Kindersley Limited
For further information see: www.dkimages.com

A WORLD OF IDEAS:
SEE ALL THERE IS TO KNOW
www.dk.com

CONTENTS

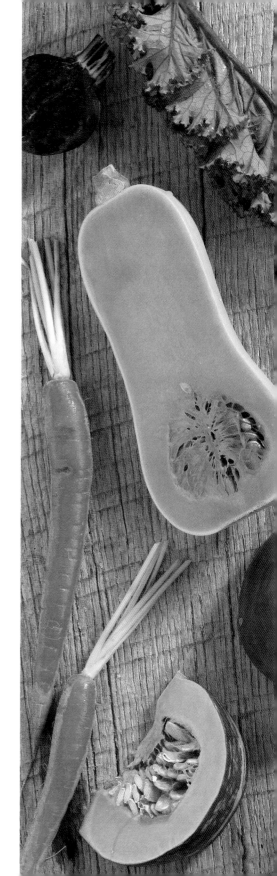

INTRODUCTION

Soup is as old as the history of cooking. Simmering simple ingredients to make nutritious and filling meals has been practised for centuries.

Be it gazpacho, vischyssoise, sweetcorn chowder, or tortilla soup, all are variations on the same theme, each having been influenced and shaped by local ingredients and traditions. In the past, there was nothing trendy about soup; it was just nutrition-based eating.

Kale, quinoa, and fresh-pressed juices have all had their moments in the spotlight. Now is the time for soup. However, I'm not talking about preservative-filled tinned soups, or cream-and-butter-rich restaurant soups. I'm talking about back to basics – to what soups were and should be. Fresh, preservative-free vegetable soups that are full of nutrients and brimming with bright flavours.

The purpose of this book is not only to offer a fresh take on what soup can be, but also to introduce soup as a lifestyle known as "souping". Souping can simply be the idea of integrating fresh, nutrient-dense soups into your daily diet to provide additional nutrition and hydration. Or, for those looking for further benefits like detoxification and alkalinity, souping can mean following a diet of these nutrient-rich soup blends for a set amount of time as a cleanse programme.

This collection of more than 75 hot and chilled soup recipes, along with 10 different cleanse programmes, aims to make souping at home easy. These carefully crafted recipes are meant to provide the right mix of nutrition, variety, and deliciousness. Souping is an easy, convenient, and delicious way to hydrate, nourish, and energize the body. You shouldn't have to go to extremes to feel the benefits of mindful eating. I am excited to share some of my favourite health blends and hope that these recipes help make eating healthy at home a little bit simpler.

Just heat, sip, enjoy, and repeat.

1
SOUPING ESSENTIALS

In this part, you'll learn what souping is and why you should make it part of your healthy lifestyle. You'll get ideas for stocking your store cupboard with essential ingredients, tips on selecting kitchen equipment, and suggestions for storing your soups in order to make souping as easy as possible.

WHAT IS SOUPING?

Souping is the idea of incorporating nutrient-dense, vegetable-based soups into your diet. Whether you embark on an all-soup cleanse or just replace one or two meals a day with soup, it's an ideal way to pump your body full of nutrients, antioxidants, and phytochemicals.

BENEFITS OF A SOUP CLEANSE

Soups are a great way to build more healthy and satisfying meals into your diet. Because soups are high in water and fibre, but low in sugar, they are filling without causing spikes in blood sugar.

The mind-body benefits of a soup cleanse are many:
★ flushes out harmful toxins
★ encourages weight loss
★ boosts immunity
★ increases energy
★ reduces cravings
★ aids digestion
★ improves gut health
★ refocuses the mind
★ eases headaches
★ brightens the skin

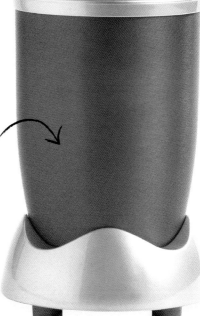

Souping uses fresh, whole ingredients that are unprocessed and nutrient dense.

Souping can help cleanse, detoxify, and energize the body.

Making soups is a simple process and only requires some basic kitchen equipment.

Souping offers an easy and convenient way to eat a wide variety of vegetables, fruits, and wholegrains.

SOUPING VS. JUICING

You may be wondering how souping compares to another popular diet trend, juicing. While juices are extracted from fruits and vegetables, leaving the fibrous pulp behind, soups are made by puréeing whole ingredients, and they retain beneficial fibre. Souping and juicing share many positive attributes, but souping is more versatile and has added health benefts, thanks to the increased fibre, fat, and protein, and fewer sweet ingredients.

SOUPING

nutrient-dense, vegetable-based soups

- ✓ Easily adaptable for diet and allergy restrictions
- ✓ Hydrating
- ✓ Low in fat and calories
- ✓ Easy to digest
- ✓ Filling and high in fibre
- ✓ Low in sugar (no blood sugar spikes)
- ✓ Includes protein from legumes, greens, and grains
- ✓ Includes healthy fats, such as coconut oil and olive oil
- ✓ Can be served hot or cold
- ✓ Variety of flavours, from savoury to sweet
- ✓ Can be made ahead and frozen

JUICING

raw juice made from fruits and vegetables

- ✓ Vegan and gluten free
- ✓ Hydrating
- ✓ Low in fat and calories
- ✓ Easy to digest
- ✓ Energizing
- ✗ Low in fibre
- ✗ May be high in sugar (natural fructose)
- ✗ Not a good source of protein or healthy fats
- ✗ Primarily served chilled
- ✗ Usually sweet, with few savoury options
- ✗ Short shelf life
- ✗ Less economical due to the volume of ingredients required

HEALTH BENEFITS OF SOUPING

A soup cleanse provides both physical and mental benefits. Wholesome, vegetable-based soups are filling and satisfying, as well as rich in beneficial antioxidants and phytochemicals.

A FRESH START

Just making the decision to cleanse is a huge step in the right direction. By breaking your normal routine, you have a definite starting point, as well as the motivation to continue with healthy habits.

A cleanse provides a set amount of time to reset and prioritize your goals going forward. By changing your diet in a focused, specific way, you become more mindful of your eating.

Detoxification
You are constantly exposed to environmental toxins. A cleanse helps flush these toxins from your body.

Weight Loss
Lifestyle and diet directly affect your weight. A calorie-controlled cleanse brings you back to basics and can help drop pounds while curbing cravings.

BODY BENEFITS

Improved Gut Health
Fibre- and nutrient-rich, a cleanse can help promote proper digestion and restore gut health.

Hydration
The body functions best with proper hydration. A cleanse dictates a schedule that will boost your body's hydration.

FOCUS ON NUTRITION

While you cleanse, you avoid foods that may be detrimental to your physical and mental wellbeing, such as refined carbohydrates, sugar, and caffeine. Instead, a soup cleanse relies on wholesome, nutrient-rich ingredients that deliver the sustenance you need. Even two or three days of souping can make a difference to your physical and mental health. Incorporating soups and soup cleanses into your diet on a regular basis can result in lasting benefits.

Improved Mood
Diet choices can affect your metabolism, hormones, and neurotransmitters, which in turn affect your emotions. A vegetable-rich cleanse that is low in sugar keeps these variables in check.

Increased Mental Clarity
Poor nutrition can lead to mental fogginess and lethargy. Both hydrating and nourishing, a cleanse can reawaken the senses.

Better Sleep
Poor nutrition and dehydration can affect the quality of your sleep. A cleanse can be restorative for the body and encourage regular sleep patterns.

MIND BENEFITS

Reduced Cravings
Cutting out sugar and processed foods through a cleanse allows you to reset your body. Withdrawal will last only a few days, after which your cravings will subside.

Fewer Headaches
Fatigue and poor hydration can lead to headaches. A cleanse restores proper hydration and nutrition.

ESSENTIAL INGREDIENTS

Healthy and delicious soups start with high-quality, nutrient-rich ingredients. Seek out organic, seasonal produce when possible, and stock up on key dry goods such as oils, spices, and legumes.

INGREDIENT Q&A

Q **What kind of salt should I use?**
A Look for mineral-rich, unrefined salts, such as sea salt. Avoid table salt, which is highly refined.

Q **Is it okay to substitute dried herbs for fresh herbs?**
A Dried herbs can be substituted for fresh herbs in cooked soups. Because dried herbs are more potent than fresh, reduce the amount by two-thirds. Avoid using dried herbs in soups that are raw or chilled.

Q **Can I use store-bought broths?**
A Store-bought broths will work in a pinch, but it's highly recommended that you make your own broth. Store-bought broths are often high in sodium and may contain MSG and other additives.

Q **What kind of onions should I use?**
A In most cases, yellow onions are the best choice. Use sweet onions for a milder flavour and red or white onions for a more pungent flavour.

Q **Can I use canned or frozen fruits and vegetables?**
A Nothing beats fresh produce, but when fresh isn't available, opt for frozen over canned. When purchasing, make sure there are no added sauces or seasonings.

Q **Should I use purified water for my soups?**
A While recommended, this is not strictly necessary. Purified water has been filtered or processed to remove trace contaminants and impurities, making it ideal for soups. Tap water may contain chlorine and other chemicals, which may reduce the health benefits of other ingredients.

Q **Where can I get bones to make my bone broth?**
A Bones can be found inexpensively at your local butcher shop, or you can save the bones after roasting a chicken or cooking bone-in cuts of meat. Wrap the bones in foil, place in a freezer bag, and freeze until ready to use.

STORE CUPBOARD

Many of the soups in this book rely on a few key ingredients. Keeping your store cupboard stocked with these staples will make it easier to shop for soups.

Spices: Have sea salt and black pepper on hand, as well as other basic spices such as red pepper flakes, cumin, and chilli powder. Store spices in tightly closed containers, away from light.

Oils: Coconut oil and olive oil are used to cook vegetables for soups. Look for cold-pressed, virgin (or extra-virgin) varieties.

Garlic: Fresh garlic should be kept in the store cupboard, not the fridge. Keep garlic bulbs loose, with airflow to prevent decay.

Onions: Onions add savoury flavour and mouth-watering aroma to many soups. Like garlic, onions are best stored in the dark, at room temperature, with plenty of airflow.

Grains: Look for less-familiar ancient grains such as quinoa, freekeh, amaranth, and millet, as these contain more protein and nutrients than white or even brown rice.

Legumes: Beans are a great way to add protein and body to soups. Keep a supply of canned or dried chickpeas and black beans on hand, as well as a stock of dried lentils.

Canned chopped tomatoes: Canned chopped tomatoes are packaged at the peak of ripeness and deliver rich umami flavour as well as lycopene. Look for low-salt varieties.

Light coconut milk: Coconut milk is shelf-stable and brings creaminess and body to both sweet and savoury soups without added dairy.

Nuts: Cashews and almonds can be soaked and blended to deliver protein and creamy texture to soups. Use raw, unsalted varieties.

Water: Water is an essential ingredient in soup making, and the type you use can make a difference. Ideally, keep a stock of purified water to get the most nutrients from your soups, but tap water is fine, too.

FRIDGE & FREEZER

Fresh produce and meats are vital to making delicious, nutrient-rich soups. These are some of the most-often used fresh ingredients in this book.

Carrots: A base for many soups is the classic mix of carrots, onions, and celery, known as mirepoix. Carrots, which are rich in vitamin A, are essential to this trio and add a slight sweetness to balance out the flavours.

Celery: Another crucial ingredient to the mirepoix mix is celery. Celery adds an aromatic note, which delivers depth and complexity of flavour.

Spinach: Iron-rich spinach has a mild flavour, which complements both sweet and savoury soups. Look for baby spinach, which is slightly sweeter with tender leaves.

Fresh herbs: Herbs introduce lots of flavour and freshness to your soups with no additional calories. Keep fresh basil, parsley, and coriander on hand.

Fresh ginger and turmeric: Fresh ginger and turmeric are inexpensive and will keep a long time. These fresh spices are nutritional powerhouses that complement a range of dishes, from savoury to sweet.

Lemons: These are a great source of vitamin C, and a squeeze of lemon can boost the nutritional content and brighten the overall flavour profile of a soup.

Chillies: Chilli peppers are a great way to add flavour without extra calories. Try poblano, jalapeño, and serrano peppers.

Coconut water: Hydrating coconut water replenishes electrolytes and makes a great base for chilled soups.

Bone-in chicken pieces and other meat bones: Animal bones are the foundation of nutrient-rich bone broths.

Home-made broths: Broth freezes well, so make a big batch when you have time and freeze it in small containers for later use.

MAKING SOUPS

One of the best things about souping is that most of the recipes come together quickly and can be prepared in advance, making it a manageable diet that doesn't require spending every evening at the stove.

TYPES OF SOUPS

Almost all of the soups in this book are puréed or strained for a smooth texture and ease of sipping on the go. Soups may be served hot or cold.

Hot Soups

Soups that are meant to be served warm or hot are typically prepared by cooking ingredients, either on the hob or roasting, and then puréeing them along with the cooking liquid.

Chilled Soups

Chilled soups may be prepared from cooked or raw ingredients. Soups that do not freeze well are often those made with raw ingredients, such as banana or melon. When making a chilled soup, be sure to allow time for refrigeration.

Broths and Consommés

These clear, thin liquids are prepared by simmering vegetables and/or meat or poultry bones in water for an extended time, allowing the beneficial minerals to be drawn out. Broths and consommés often include aromatics, such as ginger, for added flavour and nutrients. Broths are simply strained before using, while consommés are clarified to remove impurities, usually by using egg whites.

TOOLS AND EQUIPMENT

Soups don't require a lot of special kitchen equipment. In addition to a blender, you'll need the following:
★ Baking sheet
★ Casserole
★ Chef's knife
★ Chopping board
★ Frying pan
★ Ladle
★ Mesh sieve
★ Paring knife
★ Peeler
★ Prep bowls
★ Spatula
★ Wooden spoon

Hot Stuff

When a recipe calls for blending hot soups, take care. The steam from the hot ingredients creates pressure that can push the lid right off the blender, splashing liquid everywhere (including on you). If you're using a regular blender, remove the centre plug from the lid and cover it with a folded dish towel while blending to prevent steam buildup. Another option is using an immersion blender. Take the cooking pot off the heat and carefully purée the ingredients in the pot.

1 PREP

A crucial aspect of souping success is allowing enough time to plan and prepare. Once you have selected a cleanse, create a master list of all the ingredients you will need for the cleanse, and shop for ingredients ahead of time. Keeping your kitchen stocked with staples will cut down on shopping time.

2 COOK AND BLEND

To make cooking manageable, it's recommended that you begin preparing soups a week ahead of your cleanse. When you are ready to cook, make sure you have the ingredients for all the soups you are making that day, along with your basic utensils. Start by prepping all the ingredients, like mincing garlic and dicing onion. Once all your ingredients are prepped, the actual cooking goes quickly.

BLENDER

A traditional blender is capable of puréeing large quantities of soup, and is able to achieve a smooth consistency, even for tough or fibrous ingredients. For the smoothest and easiest blending, you may consider investing in a high-powered blender.

IMMERSION BLENDER

A handheld immersion blender allows you to purée soups right in the pot that you used for cooking. Immersion blenders are great for safely puréeing hot ingredients, and they also cut down on dishes to wash.

BULLET STYLE BLENDER

A bullet-style blender is useful for making single servings of soups, especially those with perishable ingredients. It's also simple to clean.

FOOD PROCESSOR

A food processor can be used in place of a blender if needed, but it may not achieve as smooth a texture, and transferring liquid ingredients to and from the bowl may be difficult.

3 STORE

If you're not eating your soup immediately, transfer it to an airtight container and store in the fridge or freezer (if the soup can be frozen). Most soups can be refrigerated for several days or frozen for up to eight weeks. To defrost frozen soups, allow them to thaw for 24 hours in the fridge. Before serving, you may want to blend your soups briefly to recombine the ingredients.

STORING SOUPS

Most soups can be prepared days or even weeks in advance, provided you store them properly. Cook in batches, and invest in a set of freezer-safe, single-serving containers for portioning and storing your soups.

COOK IN BATCHES

It takes almost the same amount of time to prepare a single batch of soup as it does to make several batches of that same soup. Save time and energy by making double or triple batches. In most cases, extra portions can be frozen for a later date. Check the storage information on the recipe for refrigeration and freezing times.

STORE IN SINGLE-SERVING PORTIONS

Rather than ladling out one serving at a time from a large container, immediately portion your soups into single-serving containers. In addition to cooling more quickly, single-serving containers make efficient use of fridge and freezer space, are easy to grab and go, and ensure that you consume the intended amount of calories.

pineapple & kale soup

strawberry chia soup

winter root vegetable soup

To minimize leaks... transport soups while frozen and thaw in a fridge or microwave at your destination.

CHOOSE THE RIGHT CONTAINER

Look for airtight, leak-proof containers that can withstand heat, so you can easily microwave your soups on the go. Your containers should be large enough to hold at least 500ml (16fl oz) of soup, with room to heat and stir. Glass Mason jars or sturdy plastic containers with screw-top lids are great for storing and transporting soups.

10 Soups to Freeze

Most of the recipes in this book freeze well. Make a double batch of one of these freezer-friendly soups to get started.

1 Black Bean Poblano Soup
2 Nutmeg Sweet Potato Soup
3 Broccoli Rocket Soup
4 Courgette Soup with Basil
5 Curried Butternut Soup
6 French Lentil Soup
7 Winter Root Vegetable Soup
8 Butternut Black Bean Soup
9 Sesame Vegetable Broth
10 Carrot & Fennel Soup

raspberry coconut soup

avocado & rocket soup

superfood berry soup

PREPARING FOR A CLEANSE

This book contains 10 soup cleanses, each of which is designed to support or nourish specific aspects of your health. Choose a cleanse that speaks to your health needs and fits your upcoming schedule.

SELECT A CLEANSE

★ Choose a time to cleanse when you don't have a lot going on in your social or work calendar.

★ Ask a friend or your partner to join you in doing your cleanse. It's always easier when you have someone to hold you accountable.

THE 10 CLEANSES

1 Metabolism Boost: Reset and boost metabolism. PAGE 34

2 Energize: Boost energy and stamina. PAGE 46

3 Weight Loss: Reduce bloating and kick-start weight loss. PAGE 66

4 Hydrate: Refresh and hydrate your body. PAGE 78

5 Alkalize: Rebalance your body's pH levels. PAGE 98

6 Beauty Reboot: Nourish your hair, skin, and nails. PAGE 110

7 Detoxify: Remove impurities from your body. PAGE 132

8 Immune Boost: Strengthen and boost your immune system. PAGE 144

9 Digestive Health: Soothe and restore natural balance to your digestive system. PAGE 164

10 Anti-Inflammatory: Reduce inflammation and combat joint pain. PAGE 176

PREPARE FOR A CLEANSE

2 WEEKS BEFORE

★ Select your cleanse.

★ Check the shopping list for your cleanse and buy any store-cupboard staples or other non-perishable items you need.

1 WEEK BEFORE

★ Make sure you have appropriate storage containers for storing your soups. If you plan to store your soups in individual portions, you will need six 500ml (16fl oz) containers for each day of the cleanse.

★ Purchase ingredients for the two soups that you will make and freeze ahead.

★ Make two soups for your cleanse and freeze them.

4 DAYS BEFORE

★ Purchase the ingredients for your remaining soups as well as healthy foods to begin transitioning your diet as you prepare for your cleanse.

3 DAYS BEFORE

★ In the three days before your cleanse, prepare the remaining four soups.

★ Start transitioning your diet as outlined in your cleanse, weaning yourself off sugars and processed foods.

CLEANSE Q&A

Q Do I have to consume the soups in a certain order?

A No. While there is a suggested order based on the health benefits of specific soups (for example, starting the day with a metabolism-boosting soup), it will not impact the outcome of the cleanse to choose a different order.

Q Can I exercise while cleansing?

A Movement and exercise are always good for the body. Just be aware that your calorie intake may be lower than usual, so you may not want to burn too many calories.

Q How will cleansing make me feel?

A Everyone's experiences differ based on what their normal diets and habits may be. Most people find the first day to be the most challenging. Some people experience lethargy or headaches. Don't worry; this is just a sign that your body has registered a change. The headaches and tiredness should abate after the first or second day of cleansing.

Q Can I drink coffee?

A Coffee is an acidic food that takes your body out of its optimal alkaline state. One of the great benefits of a souping cleanse is that it will help curb cravings. For the short time you cleanse, try to forego coffee. If you really need caffeine, try green tea.

Q Can I freeze the soups?

A The majority of the soups in this book can be frozen. Look for freezing instructions in the Storage section of the recipe. (Defrost frozen soups for 24 hours in the fridge before serving.)

Q Can I eat solid foods while cleansing?

A If you feel the need to chew or eat other foods while cleansing, try raw or steamed veggies with a squeeze of lime, or half an avocado with a sprinkle of sea salt.

Q Will I lose weight?

A Whether or not you lose weight depends on what your diet is normally; however, because the cleanses are low in calories, many people do experience weight loss.

Q Will I be hungry?

A Most people find that they are not hungry at all; in fact, some people have trouble finishing all their soups in a day. The fibre from the vegetables and the high volume of water make for a very filling combination.

Q Will cleansing slow my metabolism?

A A soup cleanse still provides sufficient calories to keep your metabolism moving. Many of the soups include ingredients that may actually speed up your metabolism.

FOLLOWING A CLEANSE

To get the most out of your cleanse, prepare your body by making slight modifications to your diet in the days leading up to and following the cleanse.

Adjusting your diet before and after a cleanse helps to maximize cleanse benefits and prevents you from returning to old habits too quickly. Whether you've curbed a craving, lost weight, gained energy, or simply kick-started a healthier lifestyle, transitioning properly can help keep the momentum going. Even if you are planning to cleanse for only a day or two, modifying your diet before and afterwards will help to ease the transition. While you're cleansing, stick to your prepared soups and avoid snacking or drinking sweetened beverages.

WHEN SHOULD I CLEANSE?	TRANSITIONING INTO A CLEANSE	DURING THE CLEANSE	TRANSITIONING OUT OF A CLEANSE
When to cleanse is entirely up to you, depending on your lifestyle and your diet. Some people like to cleanse quarterly to reboot the body as the seasons change. Others prefer monthly cleanses. Some people cleanse after a particularly indulgent weekend or holiday.	**3 Days Before:** Begin removing processed food from your diet and focus on eating whole foods, including vegetables, legumes, lean meats, and grains.	★ Try to eat only the soups you've prepared for your cleanse.	**1 Day After:** Start with a vegetable-based diet supplemented with legumes, grains, and nuts. Drink at least 8 glasses of water.
If weight loss is your goal, you may choose to cleanse more frequently over a shorter period of time. There is no right or wrong time to cleanse. Listen to your body. A nutrient-dense, vegetable-based diet is always a smart idea.	**2 Days Before:** Begin removing meat, poultry, and dairy products from your diet. Focus on a vegetable-heavy diet supplemented with fish, grains, and legumes.	★ Drink 1–2 glasses of water or unsweetened tea between each soup. (Aim for 8 glasses of water per day.)	**2 Days After:** Continue to focus on a vegetable-based diet supplemented by grains and legumes. Begin to add fish to your diet, if this is something you'd like to include. Drink at least 8 glasses of water.
	1 Day Before: Remove all animal products from your diet and focus on a vegetable-based diet supplemented with legumes, grains, and nuts. Drink at least 8 glasses of water.	★ Engage in light exercise daily.	**3 Days After:** Continue to focus on a vegetable-based diet supplemented by grains and legumes. If you'd like to add other lean proteins, like chicken or pork, do so. Drink at least 8 glasses of water.
		★ Sleep for 7–8 hours each night.	

The vegetable- and broth-based soups in this book are designed to keep you full during your cleanse while delivering key nutrients and antioxidants.

Low-sugar, high-volume soups keep you full and curb cravings.

2
SPRING SOUPING

Spring souping features cleanses for boosting your metabolism and energizing your body. The bright flavours of the spring harvest are highlighted in these recipes, which are lighter in texture yet still incredibly satisfying. The minimal ingredients in these soups allow the delicate flavours of spring to shine.

Serrano chillies boost metabolism and contain capsaicin, which helps combat cell destruction.

Mangoes are high in fibre, vitamin C, vitamin A, and iron.

MANGO SOUP WITH LIME

Mangoes give this **light, refreshing elixir** smoothness and body, as well as a **creamy texture**. The sweet mango is balanced by the **tartness of lime juice** and **mild heat of serrano pepper**. Serve chilled.

PREP & COOK
35 minutes

QUANTITY
Makes 1 litre (1¾ pints)
Serving size 500ml (16fl oz)

STORAGE
Refrigerated 5 days
Frozen 8 weeks

INGREDIENTS

2 large mangoes, peeled and cubed

¼ serrano pepper, seeds removed and finely chopped

Juice of 1 lime

750ml (1¼ pints) water

METHOD

1 Place mangoes, serrano pepper, lime juice, and water in blender. Purée for 30 seconds, or until smooth.

2 Transfer blending vessel to fridge for 30 minutes to chill. Blend briefly before serving, if needed.

NUTRITION PER SERVING

calories	214
total fat	2g
cholesterol	0mg
sodium	5mg
carbohydrate	54g
dietary fibre	6g
sugars	47g
protein	3g

To make...
Creamy Mango Soup, add 140g (5oz) Greek yogurt and 1 tsp fresh grated ginger to the blender.

Cucumber's high water and fibre content make it both hydrating and great for digestion.

AVOCADO & ROCKET SOUP

With **creamy avocado, spicy rocket,** and **hydrating cucumber,** this refreshing soup has a **smooth, silky texture** highlighted by herbal notes of **fresh basil** and **coriander.** Serve chilled.

 PREP & COOK
10 minutes

 QUANTITY
Makes 1 litre (1¾ pints)
Serving size 500ml (16fl oz)

 STORAGE
Refrigerated 5 days
Frozen 8 weeks

INGREDIENTS

½ avocado, skin and stone removed

225g (8oz) cucumber, peeled and sliced

85g (3oz) baby rocket

75g (2½oz) Little Gem lettuce, roughly chopped

15g (½oz) coriander, stems removed, finely chopped

2 tbsp basil, finely chopped

1½ tbsp red wine vinegar

600ml (1 pint) water

¼ tsp salt

⅛ tsp pepper

METHOD

1 Place avocado, cucumber, rocket, Little Gem lettuce, coriander, basil, red wine vinegar, and water in blender. Purée for 30 seconds, or until smooth.

2 If desired, transfer blending vessel to fridge for 30 minutes to chill. Season with salt and pepper and blend briefly to recombine ingredients.

NUTRITION PER SERVING

calories	89
total fat	6g
cholesterol	0mg
sodium	303mg
carbohydrate	7g
dietary fibre	4g
sugars	3g
protein	2g

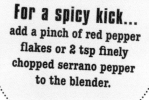

For a spicy kick...
add a pinch of red pepper flakes or 2 tsp finely chopped serrano pepper to the blender.

Almond milk contains energy-boosting riboflavin and vitamin E, which helps boost immunity.

Goji berries are high in antioxidants, fibre, and iron.

SUPERFOOD BERRY SOUP

This **sweet and slightly tart** soup is a delicious way to start the day. Creamy Greek yogurt provides a **protein-rich base,** while strawberries and goji berries add a **fruity tang.** Serve chilled.

 PREP & COOK
20 minutes

 QUANTITY
Makes 750ml (1¼ pints)
Serving size 500ml (16fl oz)

STORAGE
Refrigerated 2 days
Frozen 8 weeks

INGREDIENTS

2 tbsp ground linseeds

3 tbsp dried goji berries

250ml (9fl oz) unsweetened almond milk

300g (10oz) strawberries, hulled and quartered

140g (5oz) Greek yogurt (2% plain)

2 tsp vanilla

2 tsp honey

METHOD

1 In a small bowl, combine ground linseeds, goji berries, and almond milk. Leave to sit for 15 minutes to allow goji berries to soften and flax to thicken.

2 Place almond milk mixture, strawberries, Greek yogurt, vanilla, and honey in a blender. Purée for 30 seconds, or until smooth.

Top with...
whole linseeds for a nutty crunch, or use frozen strawberries for a thicker consistency.

NUTRITION PER SERVING	
calories	308
total fat	8g
cholesterol	6mg
sodium	218mg
carbohydrate	46g
dietary fibre	8g
sugars	32g
protein	14g

In addition to being high in vitamin C, peppers are a good source of vitamin B6, which helps detoxify the liver.

KALE & PEPPER SOUP

This mellow soup blends **mild yellow peppers, smooth avocado,** and **crisp cucumber** with **nutrient-dense kale** for a **refreshingly light** and simple **spring meal.** Serve chilled.

 PREP & COOK
20 minutes

 QUANTITY
Makes 1 litre (1¾ pints)
Serving size 500ml (16fl oz)

 STORAGE
Refrigerated 5 days
Freezing not recommended

INGREDIENTS

300g (10oz) cucumber, peeled and diced

350g (12oz) yellow pepper, diced

45g (1½oz) kale, stems removed and roughly chopped

75g (2½oz) celery, diced

30g (1oz) basil, chopped

2 tsp lemon juice

½ avocado

500ml (16fl oz) water

⅛ tsp salt

⅛ tsp pepper

METHOD

1 In a blender, combine cucumber, yellow pepper, kale, celery, basil, lemon juice, avocado, and water.

2 Purée for 30 seconds, or until smooth. Season with salt and pepper and blend briefly to combine.

NUTRITION PER SERVING

calories	154
total fat	8g
cholesterol	0mg
sodium	341mg
carbohydrate	19g
dietary fibre	8g
sugars	9g
protein	4g

For a heartier soup...
add 45g (1½oz) cooked quinoa, millet, or amaranth to blender with other ingredients.

METABOLISM BOOSTER
3-DAY CLEANSE

Metabolism is the process the body uses to break down nutrients to produce energy. A healthy metabolism helps to maintain a normal body weight, keep bodily processes functioning, and ward off fatigue. Poor diet choices can directly affect your metabolism. Use this cleanse to reboot and maintain metabolic health.

Follow for 3 days. After your cleanse, try incorporating these metabolism-boosting soups into your daily diet for continued metabolic health.

Shopping List

Fridge/Freezer

Serrano pepper (1)
Poblano pepper (1)
Onions (6 medium)
Carrot (3 medium)
Celery (4 stalks)
Garlic (19 cloves)
Fresh ginger (3 x 2.5cm/1in pieces)
Butternut squash (2 small)
Baby spinach (175g/6oz)
Mangoes (2)
Limes (9)
Fresh coriander (1 bunch)
Parsley (5 stalks)

Store cupboard

Olive oil (120ml/4fl oz)
Raw almonds (150g/5½ oz)
Agave nectar (4 tbsp)
Light coconut milk (250ml/9fl oz)
Diced tomatoes (2 x 400g cans)
Tomato purée (60g/2oz + 1 tbsp)
Chickpeas (2 x 400g cans)
Black beans (400g can)
Water (10 litres/17.5 pints)
Loose-leaf black tea, decaffeinated (2 tbsp)
Vanilla (2 tsp)
Cumin (2 tbsp + 2 tsp)
Cinnamon (1 tbsp + ½ tsp)
Cayenne (½ tsp)
Paprika (1 tsp)
Curry powder (2 tsp)
Cinnamon sticks (2)
Star anise (1)
Ground cardamom (¾ tsp)
Ancho chilli powder (1 tbsp + 1½ tsp)
Chile de árbol (3 tbsp)
Chilli powder (½ tbsp)
Salt
Pepper

PREPARATION

DURING THE CLEANSE

1 WEEK BEFORE

★ Make **Vuelve a la Vida Broth** (single batch); freeze in 500ml (16fl oz) portions. RECIPE PAGE 182

★ Make **Black Bean Poblano Soup** (single batch); freeze in 500ml (16fl oz) portions. RECIPE PAGE 102

★ Eliminate processed foods and sugar from your diet and focus on whole foods.

3 DAYS BEFORE

★ Make **Curried Butternut Soup** (double batch); refrigerate in 500ml (16fl oz) portions. RECIPE PAGE 91

★ Make **Spiced Chickpea Soup** (double batch); refrigerate in 500ml (16fl oz) portions. RECIPE PAGE 137

★ Eliminate poultry, meat, and dairy from your diet.

★ Focus on vegetable-based meals supplemented with fish, grains, and legumes.

1 DAY BEFORE

★ Make **Mango Soup with Lime** (double batch); refrigerate in 500ml (16fl oz) portions. RECIPE PAGE 27

★ Make **Chai Spiced Almond Soup** (double batch); refrigerate in 250ml (9fl oz) portions. RECIPE PAGE 140

★ Transfer Vuelve a la Vida Broth and Black Bean Poblano Soup from freezer to fridge to thaw.

★ Eliminate all animal products from your diet.

★ Eat vegetable-based meals with some legumes, grains, and nuts.

★ Drink at least 8 glasses of water.

DAILY SOUPS

BREAKFAST
Mango Soup with Lime (500ml/16fl oz)

SNACK
Vuelve a la Vida Broth (500ml/16fl oz)

LUNCH
Black Bean Poblano Soup (500ml/16fl oz)

SNACK
Curried Butternut Soup (500ml/16fl oz)

DINNER
Spiced Chickpea Soup (500ml/16fl oz)

DESSERT
Chai Spiced Almond Soup (250ml/9fl oz)

ALTERNATIVES
Cantaloupe Jalapeño Soup (breakfast) RECIPE PAGE 61

Jalapeño Chicken Broth (snack) RECIPE PAGE 156

CLEANSE BOOSTERS

★ Drink 2 glasses of alkalized water between meals.

★ Perform 30–60 minutes of moderate exercise daily during cleanse, particularly HIIT routines or weight training.

★ You may choose to receive a colonic treatment halfway through or at the end of your cleanse if you find them helpful.

KIWI KALE GAZPACHO

Slightly **tart and refreshing,** this soup features a variety of **vitamin-packed** fruits and leafy greens. **Sweet grapes** and **tangy kiwi** balance the earthier flavours of spinach and kale. Serve chilled.

PREP & COOK
10 minutes

QUANTITY
Makes 500ml (16floz)
Serving size 250ml (9fl oz)

STORAGE
Refrigerated 5 days
Frozen 8 weeks

INGREDIENTS

2 kiwi fruit, peeled and chopped

30g (1oz) kale, chopped and stems removed

85g (3oz) green grapes, halved

45g (1½oz) baby spinach

120ml (4fl oz) water

2 tsp agave nectar

METHOD

1 Place kiwi, kale, grapes, spinach, water, and agave nectar in blender. Purée for 30 seconds, or until smooth.

2 If desired, transfer blending vessel to fridge to chill for 30 minutes. Blend briefly before serving.

NUTRITION PER SERVING

calories	114
total fat	1g
cholesterol	0mg
sodium	16mg
carbohydrate	27g
dietary fibre	4g
sugars	19g
protein	2g

For best flavour...
use cavalo nero (also called lacinato kale or Tuscan kale). It tends to be less bitter than other varieties of kale.

The vitamin C in kiwi is vital to a healthy immune system.

CURRIED CARROT SOUP

Coconut milk and curry pair with **sweet carrots** and **spicy ginger** in this **savoury, warming soup.** Rich in vitamins A and C, this soup is both nutritious and restorative. Serve hot.

PREP & COOK
30 minutes

QUANTITY
Makes 1 litre (1¾ pints)
Serving size 500ml (16fl oz)

STORAGE
Refrigerated 5 days
Frozen 8 weeks

INGREDIENTS

¾ tbsp coconut oil

115g (4oz) onion, diced

¾ tsp garlic, crushed

300g (10oz) carrot, peeled and diced

1 litre (1¾ pints) water

1 tsp curry powder

4 tbsp light coconut milk

¼ tsp fresh ginger, grated

⅛ tsp salt

⅛ tsp pepper

METHOD

1 In a medium pot, heat coconut oil over medium heat for 2 minutes.

2 Add onion and garlic and cook for 5 minutes, or until garlic is fragrant and onions are translucent.

3 Add carrots and water to pot, increase heat, and bring to the boil. Reduce heat, cover, and simmer until carrots are tender, about 10 minutes.

4 Transfer contents of pot to blender and add curry powder, coconut milk, and grated ginger. Carefully blend for 30 seconds, or until smooth. Add salt and pepper to taste.

NUTRITION PER SERVING

calories	166
total fat	9g
cholesterol	0mg
sodium	242mg
carbohydrate	22g
dietary fibre	7g
sugars	10g
protein	3g

Stir in...
1 tbsp chia seeds just before serving for added protein and texture.

COURGETTE POBLANO SOUP

The **smoky, mildly spicy poblano** pepper shines in this recipe, while fibre-rich courgettes provides a silky base. **Lime and cumin** round out the **Latin flavour** of this **zesty, satisfying soup.** Serve hot.

PREP & COOK
25 minutes

QUANTITY
Makes 1.5 litres (2¾ pints)
Serving size 500ml (16fl oz)

STORAGE
Refrigerated 5 days
Frozen 8 weeks

INGREDIENTS

1½ tsp coconut oil

150g (5oz) onion, diced

2 tsp serrano pepper, chopped

350g (12oz) poblano pepper, diced and seeds removed

25g (scant 1oz) sweetcorn kernels

600g (1lb 5oz) courgettes, chopped

1.2 litres (2 pints) water

30g (1oz) coriander, chopped, stems removed

Juice of 2 limes

½ tsp cumin

⅛ tsp salt

⅛ tsp pepper

METHOD

1 In a medium pot, heat coconut oil over medium heat for 2 minutes. Add onion, serrano, and poblano. Cook until onion is translucent, about 5 minutes.

2 Add sweetcorn, courgettes, and water and bring to the boil. Reduce heat and simmer for 7 minutes, or until vegetables are cooked through. Remove from heat.

3 Transfer contents of pot to blender and add coriander, lime juice, and cumin. Purée for 30 seconds, or until smooth, adding water to thin as needed. Season with salt and pepper.

NUTRITION PER SERVING

calories	167
total fat	3g
cholesterol	0mg
sodium	140mg
carbohydrate	33g
dietary fibre	8g
sugars	17g
protein	7g

BEETROOT & ORANGE SOUP

This ruby-hued soup combines the **subtle earthiness** of beetroot with the **bright sweetness** of orange and **herbal notes** of fresh basil for a meal that is both **detoxifying and energizing.** Serve chilled.

 **PREP & COOK**
1 hour 15 minutes

 QUANTITY
Makes 1 litre (1¾ pints)
Serving size 500ml (16fl oz)

 STORAGE
Refrigerated 4 days
Frozen 8 weeks

INGREDIENTS

2 medium beetroots, ends removed

1 tbsp olive oil

350ml (12fl oz) freshly squeezed orange juice

1 tsp red onion, chopped

30g (1oz) fresh basil, finely chopped

1 tsp fresh ginger, grated

250ml (9fl oz) water

METHOD

1 Preheat oven to 450°F (230°C/Gas 8). Line a baking tray with foil. Place beetroots on prepared baking tray, drizzle with olive oil, and roast for 20–45 minutes, or until cooked through and fork-tender.

2 Remove beetroots from oven, carefully peel, and cut into cubes. (You should have about 400g/14oz roasted beetroots.)

3 In a blender, combine roasted beetroot, orange juice, onion, basil, ginger, and water. Purée for 30 seconds.

4 Transfer blending vessel to fridge for 30 minutes, or until chilled. Blend briefly to recombine ingredients and serve immediately.

NUTRITION PER SERVING

calories	183
total fat	7g
cholesterol	0mg
sodium	66mg
carbohydrate	29g
dietary fibre	3g
sugars	21g
protein	3g

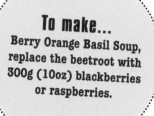

To make...
Berry Orange Basil Soup,
replace the beetroot with
300g (10oz) blackberries
or raspberries.

Beetroot is high in folate, which is vital to healthy cell growth.

SPINACH & WHITE BEAN SOUP

Hearty and filling, this soup features a savoury base of onion, carrot, and celery, with **white beans for body and protein.** Fresh basil, garlic, and lemon complement the **earthy greens.** Serve hot.

 PREP & COOK
35 minutes

 QUANTITY
Makes 1.5 litres (2¾ pints)
Serving size 500ml (16fl oz)

 STORAGE
Refrigerated 5 days
Frozen 8 weeks

INGREDIENTS

¾ tbsp olive oil

115g (4oz) onion, diced

115g (4oz) carrot, diced

115g (4oz) celery, diced

3 garlic cloves, crushed

1 tbsp tomato purée

1.2 litres (2 pints) water

2 x 400g cans white beans
  beans, drained and rinsed

175g (6oz) baby spinach

60g (2oz) kale, roughly
  chopped

¼ tsp red pepper flakes

3 tbsp fresh basil, chopped

1 tsp lemon juice

⅛ tsp salt

⅛ tsp pepper

METHOD

1 In a medium pot, heat olive oil over medium heat for 2 minutes, or until shimmering.

2 Add onion, carrots, celery, and garlic and cook for 5 minutes, or until garlic is fragrant and onions are translucent. Add tomato purée and cook for another 5 minutes.

3 Add water and beans, increase heat, and bring to the boil. Reduce heat and simmer for 10 minutes. Stir in spinach and kale and allow to wilt.

4 Carefully transfer contents of pot to blender. Add red pepper flakes, basil, and lemon juice. Purée for 30 seconds, or until smooth. Season with salt and pepper.

Instead of water... use chicken bone broth for a richer flavour profile and added health benefits.

NUTRITION PER SERVING

calories	262	carbohydrate	48g
total fat	2g	dietary fibre	11g
cholesterol	0mg	sugars	5g
sodium	171mg	protein	15g

SPRING VEGETABLE SOUP

A **slow-simmered vegetable broth** forms the base of this delicate soup. **Shaved carrot** and **thinly sliced fennel** mingle with baby spinach and spring peas for the **perfect light afternoon meal.** Serve hot.

 **PREP & COOK**
1 hour 35 minutes

 QUANTITY
Makes 1 litre (13 /4 pints)
Serving size 500ml (16fl oz)

 STORAGE
Refrigerated 5 days
Frozen 8 weeks

INGREDIENTS

For Vegetable Broth:

2 tsp olive oil

115g (4oz) onion, roughly chopped

115g (4oz) carrot, roughly chopped

75g (2½oz) celery, roughly chopped

3 garlic cloves, peeled

2 litres (3½ pints) water

60g (2oz) parsley, stalks and leaves, lightly packed

For Soup:

2 tsp olive oil

175g (6oz) leek, rinsed and diced

1 tsp garlic, crushed (about 1 clove)

15g (½oz) carrot, peeled into long strips

20g (¾oz) fennel, cut into 5-mm (¼-inch) slices

85g (3oz) baby spinach, tightly packed

4 tbsp frozen green peas

⅛ tsp salt

⅛ tsp pepper

METHOD

1 To make vegetable broth, in a medium casserole, heat olive oil over medium heat for 2 minutes. Add onion, carrots, celery, and garlic and cook for 5 minutes, or until onions are translucent. Add water and parsley. Cover, raise heat to high, and bring to the boil.

2 Reduce heat and simmer for 45 minutes to an hour. Strain vegetables from broth. (Vegetables can be discarded.)

3 To make soup, in a medium casserole, heat olive oil over medium heat for 2 minutes. Add leek and garlic and cook until leek is soft, about 4 minutes.

4 Add vegetable broth, carrot, fennel, spinach, and frozen peas. Continue to cook over medium heat until vegetables are cooked through, about 5 minutes. Season with salt and pepper.

NUTRITION PER SERVING

calories	130	carbohydrate	24g
total fat	3g	dietary fibre	7g
cholesterol	0mg	sugars	9g
sodium	283mg	protein	5g

STRAWBERRY CHIA SOUP

Start your day with this **slightly sweet and refreshing** combination.
Chia provides **filling protein,** strawberries contribute **key antioxidants,**
and fennel lends **a savoury balance.** Serve chilled.

 **PREP & COOK**
8 minutes

 QUANTITY
Makes 1 litre (1¾ pints)
Serving size 500ml (16fl oz)

 STORAGE
Refrigerated 4 days
Frozen 8 weeks

INGREDIENTS

175g (6oz) fennel, diced

300g (10oz)
    strawberries, hulled
    and halved

500ml (16fl oz) coconut
    water

1½ tsp agave nectar

2 tsp chia seeds

METHOD

1 In a blender, combine fennel, strawberries, coconut water,
and agave nectar. Purée for 30 seconds, or until smooth.

2 Stir in chia seeds and leave to sit for 10 minutes, or until
soup is slightly thickened.

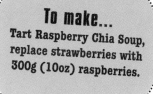

To make...
Tart Raspberry Chia Soup,
replace strawberries with
300g (10oz) raspberries.

NUTRITION PER SERVING

calories	187
total fat	4g
cholesterol	0mg
sodium	301mg
carbohydrate	36g
dietary fibre	12g
sugars	31g
protein	5g

ENERGIZE
3-DAY CLEANSE

The soups in this cleanse are packed with ingredients that both boost energy and provide sustenance for long periods of time, making it the perfect cleanse for times you're feeling lethargic or depleted.

Follow for 3 days. After your cleanse, try incorporating these energy-boosting soups into your diet when you need an extra lift.

Shopping List

Fridge/Freezer
Carrots (11 medium)
Celery (10 stalks)
Kale, chopped (60g/2oz)
Baby spinach (350g/12oz)
Mushrooms (225g/8oz)
Celeriac (2 bulbs)
Onion (1.5kg/3lb 3oz)
Granny Smith apples (3)
Strawberries (600g/1lb 5oz)
Oranges (3)
Grapefruits (2)
Lemons (10)
Lemon juice (1 tsp)
Garlic (17 cloves)
Chives (60g/2oz + 6 tbsp)
Basil, chopped (3 tbsp)
Fresh parsley (85g/3oz)
Lavender, chopped (2 tsp)
Unsweetened almond milk (500ml/16fl oz)
Greek yogurt, 2% plain (280g/9½oz)

Store cupboard
Coconut water (150ml/5fl oz)
Coconut oil (3 tbsp)
Olive oil (300ml/½ pint)
Water (6.25 litres/11 pints)
Tamari (4 tbsp)
Vanilla extract (2 tsp)
Honey (2 tsp)
Linseeds, ground (4 tbsp)
Chia seeds (2 tbsp)
Goji berries, dried (6 tbsp)
Freekeh (85g/3oz dry)
Tomato purée (1 tbsp)
White beans (2 x 400g cans)
Red pepper flakes (¼ tsp)
Dried parsley (2 tbsp)
Bay leaves (2)
Salt
Pepper

PREPARATION

DURING THE CLEANSE

1 WEEK BEFORE	3 DAYS BEFORE	1 DAY BEFORE	DAILY SOUPS	CLEANSE BOOSTERS

★ Make **Tamari & Lemon Broth** (double batch); freeze in 500ml (16fl oz) portions. RECIPE PAGE 171

★ Make **Spinach & White Bean Soup** (single batch); freeze in 500ml (16fl oz) portions. RECIPE PAGE 42

★ Eliminate processed foods and sugar from your diet and focus on whole foods.

★ Make **Carrot Soup with Chives** (double batch); refrigerate in 500ml (16fl oz) portions. RECIPE PAGE 52

★ Make **Apple & Celeriac Soup** (triple batch); refrigerate in 500ml (16fl oz) portions. RECIPE PAGE 109

★ Eliminate poultry, meat, and dairy from your diet.

★ Focus on vegetable-based meals supplemented with fish, grains, and legumes.

★ Make **Superfood Berry Soup** (double batch); refrigerate in 500ml (16fl oz) portions. RECIPE PAGE 31

★ Make **Citrus Soup with Lavender** (single batch); refrigerate in 250ml/9fl oz portions. RECIPE PAGE 150

★ Transfer Tamari & Lemon Broth and Spinach & White Bean Soup from freezer to fridge to thaw.

★ Eliminate all animal products from your diet.

★ Eat vegetable-based meals with some legumes, grains, and nuts.

★ Drink at least 8 glasses of water.

BREAKFAST
Superfood Berry Soup (500ml/16fl oz)

SNACK
Tamari & Lemon Broth (500ml/16fl oz)

LUNCH
Carrot Soup with Chives (500ml/16fl oz)

SNACK
Apple & Celeriac Soup (500ml/16fl oz)

DINNER
Spinach & White Bean Soup (500ml/16fl oz)

DESSERT
Citrus Soup with Lavender (250ml/9fl oz)

ALTERNATIVES
Apple & Amaranth Soup (breakfast)
RECIPE PAGE 100

Banana Walnut Soup (snack)
RECIPE PAGE 107

★ Drink 2 glasses of alkalized water between meals.

★ Perform 20–30 minutes of light to moderate exercise daily.

★ You may choose to receive a colonic treatment halfway through or at the end of your cleanse if you find them helpful.

GINGER GREENS SOUP

Coconut milk gives this **light and hydrating combination** a silky texture, which is accented by a **touch of ginger.** Cos and spinach lend a **fresh, vegetal flavour** and deep, verdant colour. Serve chilled.

PREP & COOK
40 minutes

QUANTITY
Makes 1 litre (1¾ pints)
Serving size 500ml (16fl oz)

STORAGE
Refrigerated 4 days
Frozen 8 weeks

INGREDIENTS

¾ tbsp olive oil
150g (5½oz) onion, diced
2 tsp garlic, crushed
   (about 2 cloves)
175g (6oz) cos lettuce,
   roughly chopped
175g (6oz) baby spinach
15g (½oz) coriander
500ml (16fl oz) water
1 tsp fresh ginger, grated
2 tbsp light coconut milk
⅛ tsp salt
⅛ tsp pepper

METHOD

1 In a medium pan, heat olive oil over medium heat for 2 minutes. Add onion and garlic, and cook until onion is translucent, about 5 minutes.

2 Transfer onion and garlic to blender. Add cos, spinach, coriander, water, and ginger. Purée for 30 seconds. Add coconut milk and season with salt and pepper. Blend until smooth.

3 Transfer blending vessel to fridge for 30 minutes, or until chilled. Blend briefly before serving to recombine ingredients.

Superfood spinach is full of nutrients, including fibre, calcium, and potassium.

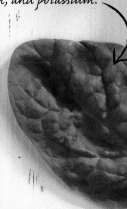

To make...
Savoury Sesame Greens Soup, add 1 tbsp tamari and ½ tsp sesame oil to the blender.

NUTRITION PER SERVING

calories	67
total fat	2g
cholesterol	0mg
sodium	195mg
carbohydrate	12g
dietary fibre	3g
sugars	5g
protein	3g

Asparagus is high in vitamin K, which helps build healthy bones and protects against heart disease.

ASPARAGUS SOUP WITH MINT

This **light, savoury soup** captures the **taste of spring**. The flavour of asparagus is highlighted by **cool mint** and **zesty lemon**. Smooth and refreshing, this soup is a **perfect afternoon boost**. Serve chilled.

 PREP & COOK
20 minutes

 QUANTITY
Makes 750ml (1¼ pints)
Serving size 500ml (16fl oz)

 STORAGE
Refrigerated 4 days
Frozen 8 weeks

INGREDIENTS

¾ tbsp olive oil

150g (5½oz) onion, diced

1 tsp garlic, crushed

225g (8oz) asparagus, trimmed and chopped

45g (1½oz) baby spinach

¼ tsp lemon zest

½ tsp mint, chopped

375ml (13fl oz) cold water

¼ tsp salt

METHOD

1 In a small pan, heat olive oil over medium heat for 2 minutes. Add onion and garlic, and cook until onion is translucent, about 5 minutes. Remove from heat.

2 Prepare an ice bath by filling a medium bowl with water and ice cubes.

3 Fill a saucepan halfway with water and bring to the boil over high heat. Blanch asparagus by submerging in boiling water for 30 seconds. Remove from heat, then drain and quickly plunge asparagus in ice bath. Leave to sit for 5 minutes.

4 Drain asparagus and add to blender along with onion, garlic, spinach, lemon zest, mint, water, and salt. Purée until asparagus is well processed and smooth.

NUTRITION PER SERVING

calories	97
total fat	2g
cholesterol	0mg
sodium	405mg
carbohydrate	18g
dietary fibre	6g
sugars	8g
protein	6g

For a heartier soup... use chicken bone broth instead of water, and top with 15g (½oz) sautéed mushrooms.

CARROT SOUP WITH CHIVES

The **ancient supergrain** freekeh lends a **nutty flavour** to this hearty soup, as well as a **boost of protein and fibre.** Top with a **swirl of chive oil** for an added savoury note. Serve hot.

 PREP & COOK
35 minutes

 QUANTITY
Makes 750ml (1¼ pints)
Serving size 500ml (16fl oz)

 STORAGE
Refrigerated 6 days
Frozen 8 weeks

INGREDIENTS

120ml (4fl oz) olive oil, plus 1 tsp

450g (1lb) yellow onion, chopped

1 tbsp garlic, crushed (about 3 cloves)

150g (5½oz) carrot, peeled and chopped

250ml (9fl oz) water

175g (6oz) freekeh, cooked

115g (4oz) chives, chopped

½ tsp salt

½ tsp pepper

METHOD

1 In a medium saucepan, heat 1 teaspoon olive oil over medium heat. Add onion and garlic and cook for 5 minutes, or until garlic is fragrant and onions are translucent.

2 Add carrots and water to saucepan and bring to the boil. Reduce heat to medium-low and simmer for 15 minutes, or until carrots are cooked through.

3 Transfer contents of saucepan to blender and add water and cooked freekeh. Purée for 45 seconds, or until smooth.

4 To make chive oil, combine chives, remaining olive oil, salt, and pepper in a clean blender. Purée until oil is smooth and chives are fully incorporated.

5 Swirl 1–2 teaspoons chive oil into soup before serving. (Leftover chive oil can be frozen for later use.)

NUTRITION PER SERVING

calories	346
total fat	8g
cholesterol	0mg
sodium	852mg
carbohydrate	64g
dietary fibre	14g
sugars	18g
protein	10g

Carrots are high in vitamin A, which helps promote strong bones and immune system health.

STRAWBERRY RHUBARB SOUP

Sweet and creamy, this blend is **reminiscent of a strawberry milkshake.** With fresh strawberries, tart rhubarb, and rich macadamia nuts, it **tastes indulgent** but delivers on nutrition. Serve chilled.

PREP & COOK
1 hour 10 minutes

QUANTITY
Makes 1 litre (1¾ pints)
Serving size 250ml (9fl oz)

STORAGE
Refrigerated 4 days
Frozen 8 weeks

INGREDIENTS

100g (3½oz) unsalted macadamia nuts

100g (3½oz) rhubarb, diced

150g (5½oz) strawberries, hulled and halved

650ml (1⅛ pints) water

2 tbsp agave nectar

⅛ tsp pepper

METHOD

1 Place macadamia nuts in a medium bowl and add hot water to cover. Leave to soak for 30 minutes to 24 hours before draining (discard soaking water).

2 In a small saucepan, bring 150ml (5fl oz) water to the boil over high heat. Add rhubarb and boil for 5 minutes, or until tender. Drain and discard boiling water.

3 In a blender, combine macadamia nuts, rhubarb, strawberries, remaining 500ml (16fl oz) water, and agave nectar, and pepper. Blend until nuts are broken down and mixture is smooth, about 45 seconds.

4 Transfer blending vessel to fridge for 30 minutes, or until chilled. Blend briefly before serving.

NUTRITION PER SERVING

calories	227
total fat	19g
cholesterol	0mg
sodium	2mg
carbohydrate	15g
dietary fibre	3g
sugars	11g
protein	2g

To make...
Nut-Free Strawberry Rhubarb Soup, omit the macadamia nuts and add 175ml (6fl oz) coconut milk yogurt to blender.

Agave nectar is less likely to cause blood sugar spikes than other sweeteners.

Macadamia nuts give this soup richness and body, as well as a nutritional boost of manganese.

3

SUMMER SOUPING

Summer souping features a weight loss cleanse and a cleanse for hydration. The vibrant flavours of summer ingredients are featured in a variety of chilled and raw soups, which will cool and hydrate your body while satisfying cravings.

BEETROOT SOUP WITH FENNEL

The **robust flavour of beetroot** is complemented by fennel, lime, and ginger in this cleansing blend. **Earthy and slightly sweet,** this soup is **rich in folate and manganese** as well as vitamin C. Serve chilled.

 **PREP & COOK**
1 hour 15 minutes

 QUANTITY
Makes 1 litre (1¾ pints)
Serving size 500ml (16 fl oz)

 STORAGE
Refrigerated 5 days
Frozen 8 weeks

INGREDIENTS

1 medium beetroot, ends removed

85g (3oz) fennel, bulb and fronds, diced

Juice of 3 limes

2 tsp mint, finely chopped

2 tsp fresh ginger, grated

600ml (1 pint) coconut water

METHOD

1 Preheat oven to 450°F (230°C/Gas 8). Line a baking tray with foil. Place beetroot on prepared baking tray, drizzle with olive oil, and roast for 30–40 minutes, or until cooked through and tender.

2 Remove beetroot from oven, carefully peel, and cut into cubes. (You should have about 200g/7oz roasted beetroot.)

3 In a blender, combine roasted beetroot, fennel, lime juice, mint, ginger, and coconut water. Purée for 30 seconds.

4 Transfer blending vessel to fridge for 30 minutes, or until chilled. Blend briefly to recombine before serving.

NUTRITION PER SERVING

calories	119
total fat	1g
cholesterol	0mg
sodium	315mg
carbohydrate	27g
dietary fibre	7g
sugars	15g
protein	4g

To make...
Citrus Fennel Ginger Soup, replace the roasted beetroot with 350g (12oz) orange or grapefruit segments.

For a refreshing tonic, try stirring a few tablespoons of soup into a glass of alkalized water.

Jalapeños are high in vitamin C, which helps build collagen, a critical connective tissue.

CANTALOUPE JALAPEÑO SOUP

In this soup, **juicy cantaloupe** pairs with **spicy jalapeño** and fresh basil to make a **refreshing combination** that reduces inflammation, **aids in digestion,** and **rehydrates the body.** Serve chilled.

 PREP & COOK
45 minutes

 QUANTITY
Makes 1.5 litres (2¾ pints)
Serving size 500ml (16fl oz)

 STORAGE
Refrigerated 4 days
Frozen 8 weeks

INGREDIENTS

950g (2lb 2oz) cantaloupe, diced

1 tsp jalapeño pepper, seeds removed and finely chopped

30g (1oz) fresh basil, chopped

500ml (16fl oz) water

2 tbsp lime juice

METHOD

1 In a blender, combine cantaloupe, jalapeño, basil, water, and lime juice. Purée for 30 seconds, or until smooth.

2 Transfer blending vessel to fridge for 30 minutes to chill. Before serving, season with salt and pepper and briefly blend to recombine ingredients, if needed.

Heat levels...
of jalapeños vary from pepper to pepper; add more or less based on the heat level of your peppers.

NUTRITION PER SERVING

calories	111
total fat	0g
cholesterol	0mg
sodium	55mg
carbohydrate	27g
dietary fibre	3g
sugars	25g
protein	3g

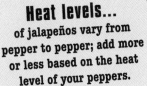

Cayenne stimulates circulation and boosts metabolic function.

RED PEPPER ROMESCO SOUP

In this summery soup, **sweet roasted peppers** are balanced by **tangy red wine vinegar** and spicy cayenne, while **protein-rich almonds** provide a **smooth, creamy texture.** Serve hot.

 PREP & COOK
17 minutes

 QUANTITY
Makes 1 litre (1¾ pints)
Serving size 500ml (16fl oz)

 STORAGE
Refrigerated 5 days
Frozen 8 weeks

INGREDIENTS

2 tbsp, plus 1 tsp olive oil

225g (8oz) onion, diced

1 tbsp garlic, crushed
(about 3 cloves)

225g can chopped tomatoes

500g (1lb 2oz) roasted red
peppers, rinsed and
drained

75g (2½ oz) blanched
almonds

⅔ tsp cayenne

2 tsp red wine vinegar

250ml (9fl oz) water

⅛ tsp salt

⅛ tsp pepper

METHOD

1 In a medium pan, heat 2 tablespoons olive oil over medium heat for 2 minutes. Add onion and garlic, and cook for 5 minutes, or until onion is translucent.

2 Transfer onion and garlic to blender. Add diced tomatoes, roasted red peppers, almonds, cayenne, red wine vinegar, water, and remaining 1 teaspoon olive oil.

3 Blend until ingredients are smooth and well combined. Season with salt and pepper and heat before serving.

NUTRITION PER SERVING

calories	308
total fat	14g
cholesterol	0mg
sodium	240mg
carbohydrate	40g
dietary fibre	12g
sugars	21g
protein	11g

For a lighter flavour...
use roasted yellow peppers
in place of roasted red
peppers.

Use summer squash
instead of courgettes
for a lighter flavour.

Spinach is loaded
with vitamin K,
which is essential
for maintaining
healthy bones.

COURGETTE SOUP WITH BASIL

Puréed courgette gives this soup a **delicate flavour** and **silky texture**, which is **enhanced by savoury onion** and floral basil. Light but satisfying, it is a **perfect summer lunch**. Serve hot.

 PREP & COOK
25 minutes

 QUANTITY
Makes 1.5 litres (2¾ pints)
Serving size 500ml (16fl oz)

 STORAGE
Refrigerated 5 days
Frozen 8 weeks

INGREDIENTS

¾ tbsp olive oil

150g (5½oz) onion, diced

2 tsp garlic, crushed
(about 2 cloves)

675g (1½lb) courgettes or
summer squash, roughly
chopped

1.5 litres (2¾ pints) water

85g (3oz) baby spinach

4 tbsp fresh basil, chopped

⅛ tsp salt

⅛ tsp pepper

METHOD

1 In a medium casserole, heat olive oil over medium heat for 2 minutes. Add onion and garlic, and cook until onion is translucent, about 5 minutes.

2 Add courgettes and water, and bring to the boil. Reduce heat and simmer for 10 minutes, or until courgettes are cooked through. Remove 500ml (16fl oz) cooking water and set aside.

3 Carefully transfer contents of pot to blender. Add spinach and basil, and purée until well combined. Add reserved cooking water as needed to reach desired consistency. Season with salt and pepper.

NUTRITION PER SERVING

calories	95
total fat	2g
cholesterol	0mg
sodium	133mg
carbohydrate	17g
dietary fibre	4g
sugars	10g
protein	5g

WEIGHT LOSS
5-DAY CLEANSE

While exercise is important when it comes to weight loss, nutrition is even more crucial. Just by making smart changes to your diet, you can impact your weight. Consistency is the key to lasting weight loss, but this cleanse is a great way to get started.

Follow for 5 days to kick-start your weight loss. Afterwards, incorporate a 3-day cleanse on a weekly basis or incorporate soups individually into your daily diet for continued weight loss.

Shopping List

Fridge/Freezer

Baby spinach (250g/9oz)
Carrots (12 medium)
Onions (9 medium)
Leeks (3)
Celery (7 stalks)
Spring onions (1 bunch)
Red pepper (2)
Poblano pepper (2)
Jalapeño pepper (1)
Sweetcorn (8 ears)
Sweet potato (1)
Butternut squash (1 small)
Parsnip (3 medium)
Fennel (1 bulb)
Cantaloupes (2 large)
Limes (8)
Parsley (1 bunch)
Basil (60g/2oz, chopped)
Garlic (38 cloves)
Fresh ginger (2 large pieces)
Lemongrass (125g/4½oz, chopped)
Fresh coriander (1 bunch)
Fresh thyme (1 tsp, finely chopped)
Frozen peas (75g/2½oz)

Store cupboard

Olive oil (175ml/6fl oz)
Toasted sesame oil (2 tsp)
Water (16 litres/3½ gallons)
Coconut oil (3 tbsp)
Tamari (6 tbsp)
Raw almonds (2 cups)
Cacao nibs (6 tbsp)
Agave nectar (2 tbsp)
Unsweetened coconut flakes (2 tbsp)
Hemp seeds (8 tbsp)
Cumin (1 tsp)
Salt
Pepper

PREPARATION

1 WEEK BEFORE

★ Make **Sesame Vegetable Broth**; freeze in 500ml/16fl oz portions. RECIPE PAGE 158

★ Make **Winter Root Vegetable Soup**; freeze in 500ml/16fl oz portions. RECIPE PAGE 131

★ Remove processed foods and sugar from your diet and focus on whole foods.

3 DAYS BEFORE

★ Make **Sweetcorn & Pepper Soup**; refrigerate in 500ml/16fl oz portions. RECIPE PAGE 76

★ Make **Spring Vegetable Soup**; refrigerate in 500ml/16fl oz portions. RECIPE PAGE 43

★ Eliminate poultry, meat, and dairy from your diet.

★ Focus on vegetable-based meals supplemented with fish, grains, and legumes.

1 DAY BEFORE

★ Make **Cantaloupe Jalapeño Soup**; refrigerate in 500ml/16fl oz portions. RECIPE PAGE 61

★ Make **Almond Cacao Soup**; refrigerate in 250ml/9fl oz portions. RECIPE PAGE 95

★ Transfer Sesame Vegetable Broth and Winter Root Vegetable Soup from freezer to fridge to thaw.

★ Eliminate all animal products from your diet.

★ Eat vegetable-based meals with some legumes, grains, and nuts.

★ Drink at least 8 glasses of water.

DURING THE CLEANSE

DAILY SOUPS

BREAKFAST
Cantaloupe Jalapeño Soup (500ml/16fl oz)

SNACK
Sesame Vegetable Broth (500ml/16fl oz)

LUNCH
Winter Root Vegetable Soup (500ml/16fl oz)

SNACK
Sweetcorn & Pepper Soup (500ml/16fl oz)

DINNER
Spring Vegetable Soup (500ml/16fl oz)

DESSERT
Almond Cacao Soup (250ml/9fl oz)

ALTERNATIVES
Watermelon Aloe Mint Soup (breakfast)
RECIPE PAGE 80

Spinach & White Bean Soup (snack)
RECIPE PAGE 42

CLEANSE BOOSTERS

★ Drink 2 glasses of alkalized water between meals.

★ Perform 45–60 minutes of moderate exercise daily during cleanse, focusing on cardio workouts.

★ You may choose to receive a colonic treatment halfway through or at the end of your cleanse if you find them helpful.

Chives contain potassium,
which helps promote
healthy kidney function.

SWEETCORN & CHIVE SOUP

This **lightly sweet purée** showcases **fresh summer sweetcorn,** which is an **excellent source of dietary fibre** and aids in digestion. Cool and refreshing, it is a **perfect light lunch** or snack. Serve chilled.

 **PREP & COOK**
1 hour 15 minutes

 QUANTITY
Makes 1.5 litres (2¾ pints)
Serving size 500ml (16fl oz)

 STORAGE
Refrigerated 4 days
Frozen 8 weeks

INGREDIENTS

2 tbsp coconut oil

300g (10oz) onion, chopped

2 tsp garlic, crushed
   (about 2 cloves)

6 ears fresh sweetcorn

1.5 litres (2¾ pints) water

1 tsp salt

½ tsp pepper

4 tbsp chives, chopped

METHOD

1 In medium casserole, heat coconut oil over medium heat. Add onion and garlic, and cook until onions are translucent, about 5 minutes.

2 Cut sweetcorn kernels from cobs. (You should have about 500g/1lb 2oz of sweetcorn.) Set aside 4 sweetcorn cobs.

3 Add water, kernels, and 4 corn cobs to pot, and bring to the boil. Reduce heat, cover, and simmer for 30 minutes.

4 Remove corn cobs and discard. Remove 250ml/9fl oz cooking water and set aside. Transfer contents of pot to blender. Purée for 30 seconds, or until smooth, adding reserved water to thin if needed. Season with salt and pepper.

5 Transfer blending vessel to fridge for 30 minutes, or until chilled. Stir in chopped chives just before serving.

NUTRITION PER SERVING

calories	293
total fat	12g
cholesterol	0mg
sodium	799mg
carbohydrate	47g
dietary fibre	5g
sugars	17g
protein	8g

To make...
Smokey Tomato & Sweetcorn Soup, add 400g (14oz) chargrilled skinned, chopped tomatoes, 2 roasted red peppers, and 1 tsp chipotle powder to blender.

PEACH SOUP WITH BASIL

With **ripe peaches** and coconut water, this **slightly sweet, herbal** combination **tastes like summer.** Lemon juice adds a tart note. For a sweeter flavour, add **a splash of agave nectar.** Serve chilled.

 PREP & COOK
10 minutes

 QUANTITY
Makes 1.5 litres (2¾ pints)
Serving size 500ml (16fl oz)

 STORAGE
Refrigerated 5 days
Frozen 8 weeks

INGREDIENTS

5 large peaches, diced
(about 475g/1lb 1oz)

30g (1oz) fresh basil,
chopped

750ml (1¼ pints) coconut
water

1 tbsp lemon juice

METHOD

1 In a blender, combine peaches, basil, coconut water, and lemon juice. Purée for 30 seconds, or until smooth.

2 If desired, transfer blending vessel to fridge for 30 minutes to chill. Blend briefly to recombine ingredients before serving.

To make...
Creamy Peach Soup with Mint, omit lemon juice, replace basil with fresh mint, and add 550g (1¼lb) Greek yogurt.

NUTRITION PER SERVING

calories	149
total fat	1g
cholesterol	0mg
sodium	65mg
carbohydrate	36g
dietary fibre	4g
sugars	31g
protein	3g

PAPAYA & SPINACH SOUP

This combination of **papaya** and **spinach** gets a nutrient boost from **spirulina,** an algae rich in protein, vitamins, and antioxidants. Lime and coriander add a **zesty, herbal** note. Serve chilled.

 PREP & COOK
5 minutes

 QUANTITY
Makes 1 litre (1¾ pints)
Serving size 500ml (16fl oz)

 STORAGE
Refrigerated 5 days
Freezing not recommended

INGREDIENTS

500g (1lb 2oz) papaya, diced

175g (6oz) baby spinach

15g (½oz) coriander, chopped and stalks removed

2 tbsp lime juice

350ml (12fl oz) coconut water

1½ tsp spirulina powder

METHOD

1 In a blender, combine papaya, spinach, coriander, lime juice, and coconut water. Purée for 30 seconds, or until smooth.

2 Add spirulina powder to blender and blend until combined. If desired, transfer blending vessel to fridge to chill for 30 minutes before serving.

NUTRITION PER SERVING

calories	158
total fat	1g
cholesterol	0mg
sodium	71mg
carbohydrate	36g
dietary fibre	4g
sugars	26g
protein	3g

HERBED CUCUMBER SOUP

With its **light, clean flavour** profile, this soup will keep you **cool and hydrated.** Fresh mint and dill add **herbal notes,** while lemon juice provides a **bright and balanced** tartness. Serve chilled.

PREP & COOK
10 minutes

QUANTITY
Makes 1.5 litres (2¾ pints)
Serving size 500ml (16fl oz)

STORAGE
Refrigerated 5 days
Frozen 8 weeks

INGREDIENTS

750g (1lb 10oz) English cucumber, peeled and chopped

750ml (1¼ pints) water

60g (2oz) spring onions, chopped

15g (1oz) fresh dill, chopped

2 tbsp fresh mint, chopped

Juice of 2 lemons

⅛ tsp salt

⅛ tsp pepper

METHOD

1 In a blender, combine cucumber, water, spring onions, dill, mint, and lemon juice. Purée for 30 seconds.

2 If desired, transfer blending vessel to fridge for 30 minutes to chill. Before serving, add salt and pepper, and blend briefly to recombine ingredients, if needed.

To make...
Creamy Cucumber Dill Soup, add 280g (9½oz) Greek yogurt and ½ tsp cumin to blender, and replace lemon juice with lime juice.

NUTRITION PER SERVING

calories	47
total fat	1g
cholesterol	0mg
sodium	263mg
carbohydrate	10g
dietary fibre	3g
sugars	5g
protein	2g

For the smoothest texture, use seedless cucumbers, or remove the seeds before puréeing.

Mint is a digestive aid as well as a natural stimulant.

PEACHES & GREENS SOUP

Sweet peaches and tangy, tropical pineapple are enhanced by mint and ginger in this refreshing, green blend. Packed with vitamins A and C as well as fibre, this soup is sure to satisfy. Serve chilled.

 PREP & COOK
15 minutes

 **QUANTITY**
Makes 1.2 litres (2 pints)
Serving size 500ml (16fl oz)

 **STORAGE**
Refrigerated 4 days
Freezing not recommended

INGREDIENTS

300g (10oz) cucumber, peeled and chopped

175g (6oz) baby spinach

175g (6oz) peach, peeled and chopped

300g (10oz) pineapple, chopped

1 tbsp fresh mint, finely chopped

1 tsp fresh ginger, grated

500ml (16fl oz) coconut water

METHOD

1 Place cucumber, spinach, peach, pineapple, mint, ginger, and coconut water in blender. Purée for 30 seconds, or until smooth.

2 If desired, transfer blending vessel to fridge for 30 minutes to chill. Blend briefly before serving.

NUTRITION PER SERVING

calories	177
total fat	1g
cholesterol	0mg
sodium	281mg
carbohydrate	41g
dietary fibre	8g
sugars	30g
protein	5g

If peaches...
are not yet in season, use 250g (9oz) diced mango instead.

ARTICHOKE BASIL SOUP

Artichokes give this soup a **luxurious, creamy texture** as well as a healthy dose of **antioxidants** and fibre. **Fragrant basil** and **zested lemon** add a crispness to this nutritional powerhouse. Serve hot.

 PREP & COOK
35 minutes

 QUANTITY
Makes 1 litre (1¾ pints)
Serving size 500ml (16fl oz)

 STORAGE
Refrigerated 4 days
Frozen 8 weeks

INGREDIENTS

1 tbsp coconut oil
50g (1¾oz) onion, diced
50g (1¾oz) carrot, diced
30g (1oz) celery, diced
1 tbsp garlic, crushed
   (about 3 cloves)
400g can artichoke hearts,
   rinsed and drained
750ml (1¼ pints) water
175g (6oz) baby spinach
30g (1oz) fresh basil,
   chopped
1 tbsp lemon zest
⅛ tsp salt
⅛ tsp pepper

METHOD

1 In a medium casserole, heat coconut oil over medium heat for 2 minutes.

2 Add onion, carrots, celery, and garlic, and cook for 5 minutes, or until onions are translucent.

3 Add artichokes and water to pot, increase heat, and bring to the boil. Reduce heat and simmer for 10 minutes. Remove and reserve 250ml (9fl oz) cooking water. Stir in spinach.

4 Transfer soup to blender and add basil and lemon zest. Carefully blend until smooth, adding reserved cooking water to thin as needed. Season with salt and pepper.

NUTRITION PER SERVING

calories	192	carbohydrate	30g
total fat	7g	dietary fibre	8g
cholestoral	0mg	sugars	1g
sodium	386mg	protein	9g

SWEETCORN & PEPPER SOUP

This **smoky, savoury combination** of fresh sweetcorn, red pepper, and poblano pepper is **reminiscent of sweetcorn chowder.** Simmering the sweetcorn cobs helps to flavour and thicken the soup. Serve hot.

PREP & COOK
40 minutes

QUANTITY
Makes 1.5 litres (2¾pints)
Serving size 500ml (16fl oz)

STORAGE
Refrigerated 5 days
Frozen 8 weeks

INGREDIENTS

1½ tbsp olive oil

150g (5½oz) onion, diced

115g (4oz) red pepper, diced

115g (4oz) poblano pepper, diced

2 tbsp garlic, crushed (about 6 cloves)

4 ears fresh sweetcorn

900ml (1½ pints) water

½ tsp cumin

3 tbsp coriander, chopped and stalks removed

⅛ tsp salt

⅛ tsp pepper

NUTRITION PER SERVING

calories	271
total fat	9g
cholesterol	0mg
sodium	152mg
carbohydrate	48g
dietary fibre	8g
sugars	14g
protein	8g

METHOD

1 In a medium saucepan, heat olive oil over medium heat for 2 minutes. Add onion, red pepper, poblano pepper, and garlic. Cook until onion is translucent, about 5 minutes.

2 Cut sweetcorn kernels from cobs. (You should have about 500g/1lb 2oz of corn.) After removing kernels, set aside 2 corn cobs.

3 Add water, sweetcorn kernels, and 2 corn cobs to pot, and bring to the boil. Reduce heat, cover, and simmer for 15 minutes, or until vegetables are cooked through and broth has thickened from the "milk" of the cobs. Remove from heat.

4 Remove corn cobs and transfer contents of pot to blender. Add cumin and coriander and purée for 30 seconds, or until smooth. Add salt and pepper and blend briefly before serving.

Top with...
toasted pepitas and sliced avocado for a more filling soup.

Red pepper contains vitamin E, which contributes to heart health.

HYDRATE
2-DAY CLEANSE

Staying hydrated is critical to keeping your body functioning at its best. While proper water intake is important, diet and lifestyle choices can also significantly impact the hydration levels of the body. If you've allowed yourself to become dehydrated, this regimen of soups will restore your body's balance.

Follow for 2 days. Get plenty of rest and avoid diuretics during the cleanse.

Shopping List

Fridge/Freezer

Celery (6 stalks)
Carrots (2 medium)
Garlic (8 cloves)
Onions (4)
Cucumbers (4)
Yellow pepper (1)
Kale (45g/1½oz, chopped)
Avocado (1)
Cauliflower (1 small head)
Sunchokes (6)
Spring onions (1 bunch)
Spinach (175g/6oz)
Lemons (7)
Pears (4)
Apples (2)
Peaches (2)
Pineapple (300g/10oz, chopped)
Parsley (1 bunch)
Fresh basil (30g/1oz chopped)
Fresh dill (15g/½oz, chopped)
Mint (3 tbsp, finely chopped)
Ginger (1 tsp, grated)

Store cupboard

Olive oil (3 tbsp)
Palm sugar (1 tbsp)
Coconut water (500ml/16fl oz)
Water (5 litres/8¾ pints)
Bay leaf (1)
Cinnamon sticks (2)
Nutmeg (1 whole)
Cayenne (¼ tsp)
Salt
Pepper

PREPARATION

1 WEEK BEFORE

★ Make **Vegetable Broth with Basil** (single batch); freeze in 500ml/16fl oz portions.
RECIPE PAGE 179

★ Make **Pear Soup with Cinnamon** (single batch); freeze in 250ml/9fl oz portions.
RECIPE PAGE 119

★ Eliminate processed foods and sugar from your diet and focus on whole foods.

3 DAYS BEFORE

★ Make **Kale & Pepper Soup** (single batch); refrigerate in 500ml/16fl oz portions.
RECIPE PAGE 33

★ Make **Roasted Artichoke Soup** (single batch); refrigerate in 500ml/16fl oz portions.
RECIPE PAGE 136

★ Eliminate poultry, meat, and dairy from your diet.

★ Focus on vegetable-based meals supplemented with fish, grains, and legumes.

1 DAY BEFORE

★ Make **Herbed Cucumber Soup** (single batch); refrigerate in 500ml/16fl oz portions.
RECIPE PAGE 72

★ Make **Peaches & Greens Soup** (single batch); refrigerate in 500ml/16fl oz portions.
RECIPE PAGE 74

★ Transfer Vegetable Broth with Basil and Pear Soup with Cinnamon from freezer to fridge to thaw.

★ Eliminate all animal products from your diet.

★ Eat vegetable-based meals with some legumes, grains, and nuts.

★ Drink at least 8 glasses of water.

DURING THE CLEANSE

DAILY SOUPS

BREAKFAST
Peaches & Greens Soup (500ml/16fl oz)

SNACK
Vegetable Broth with Basil (500ml/16fl oz)

LUNCH
Roasted Sunchoke Soup (500ml/16fl oz)

SNACK
Herbed Cucumber Soup (500ml/16fl oz)

DINNER
Kale & Pepper Soup (500ml/16fl oz)

DESSERT
Pear Soup with Cinnamon (250ml/9fl oz)

ALTERNATIVES
Avocado & Rocket Soup (dinner)
RECIPE PAGE 29

Almond Cacao Soup (dessert)
RECIPE PAGE 95

CLEANSE BOOSTERS

★ Drink 2 glasses of alkalized water between meals.

★ Sit in steam room for 15–20 minutes per day during your cleanse.

★ Get 7–8 hours of restful sleep nightly.

WATERMELON ALOE MINT SOUP

The **light, fruity flavour of watermelon** meets **cooling aloe** in this wonderfully **refreshing and hydrating** soup. This blend **promotes healthy digestion** and reduces chronic inflammation. Serve chilled.

PREP & COOK
10 minutes

QUANTITY
Makes 1 litre (1¾ pints)
Serving size 500ml (16fl oz)

STORAGE
Refrigerated 5 days
Freezing not recommended

INGREDIENTS

500g (1lb 2oz)
    watermelon, diced

Juice of 4 small lemons

2 tbsp mint, chopped

250ml (9fl oz) pure aloe
    juice

METHOD

1 In a blender, combine watermelon, lemon juice, mint, and aloe juice. Purée for 30 seconds, or until smooth.

2 Serve immediately, or transfer blending vessel to fridge to chill. Blend briefly to recombine ingredients before serving.

NUTRITION PER SERVING

calories	110
total fat	0g
cholesterol	0mg
sodium	58mg
carbohydrate	29g
dietary fibre	2g
sugars	16g
protein	2g

For added protein... stir in 2 tbsp chia seeds after blending. Leave to sit for 10 minutes to allow chia seeds to plump.

Garnish with mint leaves for added digestive benefits.

The vitamin C and antioxidants in lemons help to support a healthy immune system.

For a silkier consistency, replace pineapple with mango.

PINEAPPLE & KALE SOUP

Sweet, juicy pineapple and nutrient-dense kale power this **tropical elixir** that both **refreshes and satisfies.** A touch of **serrano pepper** gives this **transformative soup** just a **hint of heat.** Serve chilled.

 PREP & COOK
10 minutes

 QUANTITY
Makes 1.2 litres (2 pints)
Serving size 500ml (16fl oz)

 STORAGE
Refrigerated 5 days
Freezing not recommended

INGREDIENTS

500g (1lb 2oz) pineapple, diced

375g (13oz) cucumber, chopped

600ml (1 pint) coconut water

85g (3oz) kale, roughly chopped

45g (1½oz) coriander, chopped and stalks removed

2 tsp serrano pepper, seeds removed and crushed

METHOD

1 In a blender, combine pineapple, cucumber, coconut water, kale, coriander, and serrano pepper. Purée for 30 seconds, or until smooth.

2 Serve immediately, or transfer blending vessel to fridge to chill for 30 minutes. Blend briefly before serving to recombine ingredients.

NUTRITION PER SERVING

calories	144
total fat	1g
cholesterol	0mg
sodium	29mg
carbohydrate	35g
dietary fibre	4g
sugars	25g
protein	4g

To determine...
the heat level of your serrano pepper, slice it in half and lightly touch the cut edge to your tongue.

Tomatoes are rich in biotin, a B-complex vitamin that helps promote healthy skin.

For a thinner soup, stir in 250ml/9fl oz tomato juice when adding water.

MIXED PEPPER GAZPACHO

The **summer flavours** of **sweet pepper** and **cucumber** are highlighted by **red wine vinegar** and **olive oil** in this delicious raw soup. A **tomato base** adds acidity and **rich flavour**. Serve chilled.

 PREP & COOK
20 minutes +
24 hours

 QUANTITY
Makes 1 litre (1¾ pints)
Serving size 500ml (16fl oz)

 STORAGE
Refrigerated 5 days
Frozen 8 weeks

INGREDIENTS

150g (5½ oz) tomatoes, chopped

85g (3oz) red pepper, chopped

85g (3oz) yellow pepper, chopped

85g (3oz) orange pepper, chopped

150g (5½ oz) cucumber, peeled and chopped

35g (1¼oz) red onion, chopped

½ tsp garlic, crushed

175ml (6fl oz) water

1 tbsp red wine vinegar

2 tsbp extra virgin olive oil

¼ tsp salt

METHOD

1 In a food processor fitted with a chopping blade, combine tomatoes, red pepper, yellow pepper, orange pepper, cucumber, and red onion. Pulse until ingredients are combined but chunky. (Process in batches if necessary.)

2 Transfer vegetable mixture to a medium nonreactive bowl. Add garlic, water, vinegar, and olive oil. Stir to combine.

3 Refrigerate for 24 hours to allow flavours to meld. Season with salt before serving.

Add...
1 tsp finely chopped serrano pepper with the other vegetables for a spicy kick and metabolic boost.

NUTRITION PER SERVING

calories	66	carbohydrate	13g
total fat	1g	dietary fibre	4g
cholestoral	0mg	sugars	8g
sodium	301mg	protein	2g

RASPBERRY COCONUT SOUP

With **yogurt and hemp seeds** for protein and fibre, this **tart and creamy** soup is the perfect morning snack. **Sweet raspberries** provide vitamin C, while **coconut flakes** add richness and body. Serve chilled.

 PREP & COOK
35 minutes

 QUANTITY
Makes 1 litre (1¾ pints)
Serving size 250ml (9fl oz)

 STORAGE
Refrigerated 4 days
Frozen 8 weeks

INGREDIENTS

750ml (1¼ pints) water

125g (4½oz)
 unsweetened coconut
 flakes

225g (8oz) raspberries

4 tbsp hemp seeds

140g (5oz) low-fat vanilla
 yogurt

½ tsp lemon zest

METHOD

1 In a saucepan over high heat, heat water until just boiling. Remove from heat.

2 In a blender, combine hot water and coconut flakes. Purée for 30 seconds, or until smooth. (A high-powered blender is recommended.)

3 Transfer blending vessel to fridge for 30 minutes, or until well chilled.

4 Once cool, add raspberries, hemp seeds, yogurt, and lemon zest to blender. Purée for 30 seconds.

NUTRITION PER SERVING	
calories	253
total fat	20g
cholesterol	2mg
sodium	28mg
carbohydrate	18g
dietary fibre	7g
sugars	8g
protein	7g

For a smoother soup... omit water and coconut flakes, and purée all ingredients with 1 litre (1¾ pints) vanilla coconut milk.

4

AUTUMN SOUPING

Autumn souping features a beauty boosting cleanse as well as an alkalizing cleanse that will help restore your body to a proper pH balance. The cozy flavours of autumn lend rich and creamy textures to recipes that are both comforting and surprisingly healthy.

If butternut squash is not available, try kabocha squash for a slightly different flavour.

CURRIED BUTTERNUT SOUP

Warming **flavours of curry, ginger,** and **serrano pepper** combine in this **creamy autumnal soup.** Sweet butternut and **rich coconut milk** are balanced with **tart lime juice.** Serve hot.

 PREP & COOK
1 hour

 QUANTITY
Makes 1 litre (1¾ pints)
Serving size 500ml (16fl oz)

 STORAGE
Refrigerated 5 days
Frozen 8 weeks

INGREDIENTS

1 small butternut squash, halved and seeds removed

1 tbsp olive oil

115g (4oz) onion, chopped

1 garlic clove, crushed

1 tsp serrano pepper, finely chopped

1 (2.5cm/1-inch) piece fresh ginger, crushed

600ml (1 pint) water

1 tsp curry powder

Juice of ½ lime

120ml (4fl oz) light coconut milk

METHOD

1 Preheat oven to 230°C (450°F/Gas 8). Line a baking tray with foil.

2 Place butternut squash cut-side down on prepared baking tray. Bake for 40 minutes, or until flesh is tender. Scoop the flesh from the skin and measure out 675g (1½lb) cooked squash (any extra can be reserved for another purpose).

3 In a medium casserole, heat oil over medium heat and add onion, garlic, serrano pepper, and ginger. Cook until onions are translucent and garlic is fragrant, about 4 minutes.

4 Add the measured butternut squash and water, increase heat, and bring to the boil. Reduce heat and simmer for 15 minutes. Remove from heat.

5 Transfer soup to blender and add curry powder, lime juice, and coconut milk. Purée for 45 seconds, or until smooth.

NUTRITION PER SERVING

calories	251	carbohydrate	41g
total fat	4g	dietary fibre	11g
cholesterol	0mg	sugars	10g
sodium	26mg	protein	4g

Cauliflower is a vitamin C powerhouse and packs a powerful antioxidant punch.

TRUFFLED CAULIFLOWER SOUP

The **velvety texture** of cauliflower and **rich flavour** of truffle oil give this healthy soup an **indulgent** feel. Leeks lend a savoury note and deliver **vitamin K** for heart and bone health. Serve hot.

 **PREP & COOK**
40 minutes

 QUANTITY
Makes 1 litre (1¾ pints)
Serving size 500ml (16fl oz)

 STORAGE
Refrigerated 5 days
Frozen 8 weeks

INGREDIENTS

1 tbsp coconut oil

175g (6oz) leek, rinsed and diced

2 tsp garlic, crushed (about 2 cloves)

450g (1lb) cauliflower, roughly chopped

1.2 litres (2 pints) water

⅛ tsp salt

⅛ tsp pepper

1 tsp truffle oil

METHOD

1 In a medium casserole, heat coconut oil over medium heat for 2 minutes. Add leek and garlic and cook until onion is translucent, about 5 minutes.

2 Add cauliflower and water to pot, increase heat, and bring to the boil. Reduce heat and simmer for 10 minutes, or until cauliflower is cooked through. Remove from heat.

3 Transfer contents of pot to blender. Purée for 30 seconds, or until well combined. Season with salt and pepper and blend briefly. Drizzle with truffle oil before serving.

NUTRITION PER SERVING

calories	130
total fat	3g
cholesterol	0mg
sodium	78mg
carbohydrate	23g
dietary fibre	6g
sugars	7g
protein	5g

For a more...
complex flavour, add a Parmesan rind to the pot while cauliflower cooks. Remove prior to blending, and finish soup with a sprinkling of chopped chives.

Almonds are alkalizing and aid in brain function.

Coconut is high in phosphorus, which helps strengthen teeth and bones.

ALMOND CACAO SOUP

Rich and satisfying, this **dessert soup** is full of **chocolatey, nutty flavour**. With healthy fats and protein from **almonds, hemp seeds, and coconut**, it's **a treat you can feel good about.** Serve chilled.

 PREP & COOK
35 minutes

 **QUANTITY**
Makes 1 litre (1¾ pints)
Serving size 250ml (9fl oz)

 **STORAGE**
Refrigerated 4 days
Frozen 8 weeks

INGREDIENTS

150g (5½ oz) raw almonds

500ml (16fl oz) water

250ml (9fl oz) coconut water

3 tbsp cacao nibs

1 tbsp agave nectar

1 tbsp unsweetened coconut flakes

4 tbsp hemp seeds

METHOD

1 Place almonds in medium bowl and cover with boiling water. Leave to sit for at least 30 minutes to soften. Drain almonds and discard soaking water.

2 In a blender, combine almonds and 500ml (16fl oz) water. Blend for 30 seconds, or until no chunks of almond remain and you are left with a creamy milk.

3 Add coconut water, cacao nibs, agave nectar, coconut flakes, and hemp seeds. Blend for 30 seconds, or until cacao is completely broken down and incorporated.

NUTRITION PER SERVING

calories	299
total fat	24g
cholesterol	0mg
sodium	15mg
carbohydrate	16g
dietary fibre	5g
sugars	8g
protein	11g

Top with...
additional hemp seeds and coconut flakes for a nutty finish and added protein.

GINGER SWEET POTATO SOUP

Sweet and spicy, this satisfying soup features nutrient-dense sweet potatoes, **rejuvenating ginger,** and **earthy turmeric.** With high levels of **immune-boosting vitamin C,** it's perfect for the cold season. Serve hot.

PREP & COOK
30 minutes

QUANTITY
Makes 750ml (1¼ pints)
Serving size 500ml (16fl oz)

STORAGE
Refrigerated 5 days
Frozen 8 weeks

INGREDIENTS

¾ tbsp coconut oil

115g (4oz) onion, diced

½ tbsp garlic, crushed

250g (9oz) sweet potato, peeled and diced

75g (2½oz) carrot, peeled and diced

500ml (16fl oz) water

1½ tbsp coconut milk

1 (2.5cm/1-inch) piece fresh ginger, grated

1 (2.5cm/1-inch) piece turmeric root, grated

½ tbsp chives, chopped

¼ tsp salt

⅛ tsp pepper

METHOD

1 In a medium casserole, heat coconut oil over medium heat for 2 minutes. Add onion and garlic and cook until onion is translucent, about 5 minutes.

2 Add sweet potato, carrot, and water. Increase heat and bring to the boil. Reduce heat and simmer for 10 minutes, or until vegetables are cooked through. Remove from heat.

3 Transfer contents of pot to blender. Add coconut milk, ginger, and turmeric, and purée until smooth. Add chives, salt, and pepper, and blend briefly before serving.

Add...
a squirt of sriracha or a few thin slices of bird's eye chilli for added heat and metabolic benefits.

NUTRITION PER SERVING

calories	174
total fat	4g
cholesterol	0mg
sodium	374mg
carbohydrate	32g
dietary fibre	6g
sugars	9g
protein	3g

Sweet potato can be replaced with butternut squash or additional carrot, if desired.

ALKALIZE
3-DAY CLEANSE

The pH of the body is directly affected by what you consume each day. A diet high in processed foods, meat, dairy, and grains causes the body to become acidic and drop below the optimal pH level of 7.4. When the pH level drops, your body is more susceptible to disease and illness. This cleanse will help restore the body's natural alkaline state.

Follow for 3 days for optimal benefits.

Shopping List

Fridge/Freezer
Garlic (8 cloves)

Onions (6)

Asparagus (1 bunch)

Baby spinach (425g/15oz)

Cos lettuce (300g/10oz)

Kale (85g/3oz, chopped)

Fresh ginger (2.5cm/1 inch piece)

Fresh sweetcorn (6 ears)

Cucumber (2 medium)

Serrano pepper (1)

Lemons (4)

Watermelon (425g/15oz, diced)

Pineapple (500g/1lb 2oz, diced)

Mint (3 tbsp, chopped)

Fresh coriander (1 bunch)

Chives (4 tbsp, chopped)

Pantry
Olive oil (3 tbsp)

Coconut oil (2 tbsp)

Aloe juice (1 litre/1¾ pints)

Coconut water (600ml/1 pint)

Light coconut milk (4 tbsp)

Water (4 litres/7 pints)

Cashews, unsalted (150g/5½oz)

Agave nectar (1 tsp)

Dried figs (40g/1¼oz)

Quinoa, uncooked (100g/3½oz)

Cardamom pods (8–10)

Vanilla pod (1)

Salt

Pepper

PREPARATION

DURING THE CLEANSE

1 WEEK BEFORE

3 DAYS BEFORE

1 DAY BEFORE

DAILY SOUPS

CLEANSE BOOSTERS

★ Make **Sweetcorn & Chive Soup** (single batch); freeze in 500ml/ 16fl oz portions. RECIPE PAGE 69

★ Make **Asparagus Soup with Mint** (double batch); freeze in 500ml/ 16fl oz portions. RECIPE PAGE 51

★ Eliminate processed foods and sugar from your diet and focus on whole foods.

★ Make **Ginger Greens Soup** (double batch); refrigerate in 500ml/16fl oz portions. RECIPE PAGE 48

★ Make **Pineapple & Kale Soup** (single batch); refrigerate in 500ml/16fl oz portions. RECIPE PAGE 83

★ Eliminate poultry, meat, and dairy from your diet.

★ Focus on vegetable-based meals supplemented with fish, grains, and legumes.

★ Drink at least 8 glasses of water.

★ Make **Watermelon Aloe Mint Soup** (single batch); refrigerate in 500ml/16fl oz portions. RECIPE PAGE 80

★ Make **Fig & Cardamom Soup** (single batch); refrigerate in 250ml/9fl oz portions. RECIPE PAGE 126

★ Transfer Sweetcorn & Chive Soup and Asparagus Soup with Mint from freezer to fridge to thaw.

★ Eliminate all animal products from your diet.

★ Eat vegetable-based meals with some legumes, grains, and nuts.

★ Drink at least 8 glasses of water.

BREAKFAST
Watermelon Aloe Mint Soup (500ml/16fl oz)

SNACK
Sweetcorn & Chive Soup (500ml/16fl oz)

LUNCH
Ginger Greens Soup (500ml/16fl oz)

SNACK
Pineapple & Kale Soup (500ml/16fl oz)

DINNER
Asparagus Soup with Mint (500ml/16fl oz)

DESSERT
Fig & Cardamom Soup (250/9fl oz)

ALTERNATIVES
Mango Soup with Lime (breakfast) RECIPE PAGE 27

Carrot & Fennel Soup (dinner) RECIPE PAGE 146

★ Drink 2 glasses of alkalized water between meals.

★ Perform 30–60 minutes of light to moderate exercise daily during cleanse. Focus on yoga or other mind-body exercises in particular, as stress can also cause acidity to build in the body.

APPLE & AMARANTH SOUP

Sweet and luxurious, this is the perfect soup for a chilly autumn morning. **Protein-rich amaranth** forms a filling base, while **warming cinnamon** adds a spicy note. Serve hot.

 PREP & COOK
25 minutes

 QUANTITY
Makes 1.2 litres (2 pints)
Serving size 500ml (16fl oz)

 STORAGE
Refrigerated 5 days
Frozen 8 weeks

INGREDIENTS

400g (14oz) Braeburn apples, peeled and diced

1 litre (1¾ pints) water

3 cinnamon sticks

125g (4½oz) cooked amaranth

METHOD

1 In a medium casserole, combine apples, water, and cinnamon sticks. Bring to the boil over high heat, and then reduce to a simmer and cover. Cook for 20 minutes, or until apples are cooked through.

2 Remove cinnamon sticks and transfer contents of pot to blender. Add amaranth and blend until smooth. Add water if needed to thin.

NUTRITION PER SERVING

calories	168
total fat	1g
cholesterol	0mg
sodium	4mg
carbohydrate	40g
dietary fibre	4g
sugars	22g
protein	3g

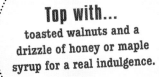

Top with...
toasted walnuts and a drizzle of honey or maple syrup for a real indulgence.

Amaranth is high in fibre and an excellent source of protein.

BLACK BEAN POBLANO SOUP

Protein-rich black beans are the foundation of this **hearty, spicy soup,** which is seasoned with **garlic** and **cumin.** Poblano peppers, along with **three types of chilli powder,** add heat and flavour. Serve hot.

PREP & COOK
50 minutes

QUANTITY
Makes 1 litre (1¾ pints)
Serving size 500ml (16fl oz)

STORAGE
Refrigerated 6 days
Frozen 8 weeks

INGREDIENTS

2 tbsp olive oil

50g (1¾oz) onion, diced

50g (1¾oz) carrot, diced

30g (1oz) celery, diced

85g (3oz) poblano pepper, diced

1 tbsp garlic, crushed (about 3 cloves)

1 tbsp tomato purée

400g can diced tomatoes

400g can black beans, drained and rinsed

1 tsp chile de árbol or cayenne powder

1 tbsp ground cumin

1 tbsp ancho chilli powder (optional)

½ tbsp chilli powder

½ tsp salt

1.5 litres (2¾ pints) water

Juice of 1 lime

2 tbsp coriander, finely chopped

METHOD

1 In a casserole, heat olive oil over medium heat. Add onion, carrot, celery, poblano pepper, and garlic. Cook until onions are translucent, about 5 minutes. Add tomato purée and toss to coat. Cook for another 5 minutes.

2 Add diced tomatoes (with liquid), black beans, chile de árbol, cumin, ancho chilli powder (if using), chilli powder, salt, and water. Increase heat and bring to the boil, then reduce heat and simmer for 20 minutes, or until water has slightly reduced and vegetables are tender.

3 Carefully transfer contents of pot to blender and add lime juice and coriander. Purée until smooth, about 45 seconds.

NUTRITION PER SERVING

calories	262
total fat	4g
cholesterol	0mg
sodium	1,727mg
carbohydrate	48g
dietary fibre	21g
sugars	7g
protein	15g

SQUASH & CRANBERRY SOUP

Sweet and savoury, this satisfying soup features **roasted winter squash** and **tart cranberries** accented with the **autumn flavours** of **ginger, rosemary,** and **maple syrup.** Serve hot.

 PREP & COOK
50 minutes

 QUANTITY
Makes 1 litre (1¾ pints)
Serving size 500ml (16fl oz)

 STORAGE
Refrigerated 5 days
Frozen 8 weeks

INGREDIENTS

2 winter squash, halved and
   seeds removed
2 tbsp olive oil
225g (8oz) onion, diced
1½ tsp garlic, crushed
2 cinnamon sticks
1.2 litres (2 pints) water
100g (3½oz) cranberries
2 tbsp pure maple syrup
2 tsp fresh ginger, grated
1 tsp fresh rosemary,
   finely chopped
¼ tsp salt
¼ tsp pepper

METHOD

1 Preheat oven to 220°C (425°F/Gas 7). Line a baking tray with foil. Place squash cut-side down on prepared baking tray. Bake for 15 minutes. Scoop flesh from skin and measure 500g (1lb 2oz) cooked squash (any extra squash can be saved for later use).

2 In a medium casserole, heat olive oil over medium heat for 2 minutes. Add onion and garlic and cook until onion is translucent, about 5 minutes.

3 Add water, measured cooked squash, and cinnamon sticks. Increase heat and bring to the boil, then reduce heat and cover. Simmer for 20 minutes. Add cranberries and simmer for another 5 minutes. Remove from heat.

4 Remove cinnamon sticks and carefully transfer contents of pot to blender. Blend until soup is smooth and ingredients are well combined. Add maple syrup, ginger, and rosemary and blend briefly. Season with salt and pepper before serving.

NUTRITION PER SERVING

calories	262
total fat	2g
cholesterol	0mg
sodium	308mg
carbohydrate	63g
dietary fibre	9g
sugars	20g
protein	4g

FENNEL & TOMATO SOUP

This **rich, savoury soup** combines **tomatoes** with aromatic fennel and **sweet carrots** to create a **hearty, warming meal** that can be enjoyed for lunch or dinner. Serve hot.

 PREP & COOK
40 minutes

 QUANTITY
Makes 750ml (1¼ pints)
Serving size 500ml (16fl oz)

 **STORAGE**
Refrigerated 5 days
Frozen 8 weeks

INGREDIENTS

1 tbsp olive oil
115g (4oz) onion, diced
2 tsp garlic, crushed
  (about 2 cloves)
175g (6oz) fennel, diced
¼ tsp fennel seeds
50g (1¾oz) carrot, diced
400g (14oz) tomato, diced
500ml (16fl oz) water
¼ tsp salt
⅛ tsp pepper

METHOD

1 In a medium casserole, heat olive oil over medium heat. Add onion and garlic and cook until onion is translucent and garlic is fragrant, about 4 minutes.

2 Add fennel, fennel seeds, and carrot, and cook until fennel is fragrant, about 2 minutes.

3 Add tomatoes and water, increase heat, and bring to the boil. Reduce heat and simmer for 20 minutes.

4 Carefully transfer contents of pot to blender. Purée until smooth, about 30 seconds. Taste and season with salt and pepper, and blend briefly to combine.

NUTRITION PER SERVING

calories	167
total fat	8g
cholesterol	9mg
sodium	360mg
carbohydrate	17g
dietary fibre	6g
sugars	9g
protein	4g

Omit fennel seeds for a more subtle fennel flavour.

APPLE & PARSNIP SOUP

Earthy, slightly **sweet parsnips** pair perfectly with **tart apples** in this smooth, **comforting soup.** Warm, **cozy vanilla** and a **hint of cinnamon** add **aroma and spice.** Serve hot.

 PREP & COOK
35 minutes

 QUANTITY
Makes 1 litre (1¾ pints)
Serving size 250ml (9fl oz)

 STORAGE
Refrigerated 5 days
Frozen 8 weeks

INGREDIENTS

1 tbsp coconut oil

115g (4oz) onion, diced

225g (8oz) parsnip, peeled and diced

1 cinnamon stick

350g (12oz) Granny Smith apple, peeled and diced

1 litre (1¾ pints) water

¾ tbsp vanilla extract, or seeds from 1 vanilla pod

⅛ tsp salt

METHOD

1 In a medium casserole, heat coconut oil over medium heat for 2 minutes. Add onion and cook until translucent, about 5 minutes.

2 Add parsnips and water to pot. Bring to the boil, reduce heat, and simmer for 5 minutes.

3 Add cinnamon stick and apples, return to the boil, and then reduce heat to simmer until apples and parsnips are cooked through, about 10 minutes.

4 Remove cinnamon stick and discard. Carefully transfer contents of pot to blender and add vanilla. Purée until smooth, about 30 seconds. Season with salt.

NUTRITION PER SERVING

calories	204
total fat	2g
cholesterol	0mg
sodium	158mg
carbohydrate	45g
dietary fibre	8g
sugars	25g
protein	2g

BANANA WALNUT SOUP

This **sweet and creamy soup** is rich in the natural sleep-aid melatonin, making it a **perfect bedtime snack.** Heart-healthy **walnuts** and **ground linseed** add richness along with **omega-3s.** Serve chilled.

PREP & COOK
12 hours

QUANTITY
Makes 1 litre (1¾ pints)
Serving size 250ml (9fl oz)

STORAGE
Refrigerated 5 days
Freezing not recommended

INGREDIENTS

750ml (1¼ pints) water

115g (4oz) walnuts

1 cinnamon stick

2 bananas, peeled and cut
    into large chunks

½ tsp vanilla extract, or
    seeds from ½ vanilla pod

2 tsp ground linseed

METHOD

1 In a saucepan over high heat, bring water to the boil. Place walnuts and cinnamon stick in a heat-tolerant bowl and cover with boiling water. Leave to cool and refrigerate overnight.

2 Remove cinnamon stick and transfer walnuts and soaking water to blender. Add bananas, vanilla, and linseed. Purée until smooth, about 30 seconds.

NUTRITION PER SERVING

calories	273
total fat	21g
cholesterol	0mg
sodium	2mg
carbohydrate	20g
dietary fibre	4g
sugars	10g
protein	6g

For a richer flavour...
try hazelnuts instead of walnuts. Macadamia nuts will provide a creamier texture.

Fresh chives are a good source of folate.

Apples are rich in vitamin C and an excellent source of fibre.

APPLE & CELERIAC SOUP

Humble celeriac is elevated when paired with **crisp apples** and **savoury onions** to make a **silky, distinctively delicious soup.** Mild and soothing, it's a comforting meal for fall. Serve hot.

 PREP & COOK
30 minutes

 QUANTITY
Makes 500ml (16fl oz)
Serving size 500ml (16fl oz)

 STORAGE
Refrigerated 5 days
Frozen 8 weeks

INGREDIENTS

1 tsp coconut oil

75g (2½oz) onion, diced

½ tsp garlic, crushed

100g (3½oz) apple, peeled and diced

150g (5½oz) celeriac, peeled and diced

500ml (16fl oz) water

⅛ tsp salt

2 tbsp chives, chopped

METHOD

1 In a medium casserole, heat coconut oil over medium heat for 2 minutes. Add onion and garlic and cook until onion is translucent, about 5 minutes.

2 Add apple, celeriac, water, and salt. Increase heat and bring to the boil, and then reduce heat and simmer for 12 minutes, or until apple and celeriac are cooked through. Remove from heat.

3 Transfer contents of pot to blender. Carefully purée until smooth, about 30 seconds. Stir in chives before serving.

NUTRITION PER SERVING

calories	255
total fat	5g
cholesterol	0mg
sodium	450mg
carbohydrate	53g
dietary fibre	9g
sugars	29g
protein	4g

To make...
Spicy Apple Celeriac Soup, omit chives and add 1 tsp chopped serrano pepper, 1 tsp grated fresh ginger, and a squeeze of lime juice.

BEAUTY REBOOT
3-DAY CLEANSE

Your diet plays a role in how you look as well as how you feel. A diet high in processed foods, sugar, refined carbohydrates, and little water can result in dull skin, dry hair, and brittle nails. Hydrating, nutrient-dense soups can help correct these issues and give your appearance a boost.

Follow for 3 days to nourish skin, hair, and nails. For a quick pick-me-up, do a 1-day cleanse programme.

Shopping List

Fridge/Freezer

Onions (6)

Carrots (10 medium)

Celery (3 stalks)

Rhubarb (60g/2oz diced)

Garlic (12 cloves)

Avocado (1)

Fennel (2 bulbs)

Cucumbers (2)

Little Gem lettuce (150g/5½oz, chopped)

Rocket (175g/6oz)

Lemon (1)

Peaches (5)

Strawberries (300g/10oz)

Parsley (1 bunch)

Fresh basil (45g,/1½oz, chopped)

Fresh coriander (30g/1oz, chopped)

Fresh thyme (1 tsp, finely chopped)

Ginger (4 tbsp, grated)

Beef bones (2kg/4lb)

Store cupboard

Olive oil (7 tbsp)

Coconut oil (4 tbsp)

Apple cider vinegar (2 tbsp)

Red wine vinegar (3 tbsp)

Chargrilled tomatoes, skins removed, seeded and chopped (200g/7oz)

Roasted red pepper (1kg/2lb 4oz)

Chickpeas, canned (165g/5¾oz)

Tomato purée (3 tbsp)

Macadamia nuts (115g/4oz)

Honey (4 tbsp)

Agave nectar (2 tbsp)

Coconut water (750ml/1¼ pints)

Water (9 litres/15¾ pints)

Bay leaf (1)

Red pepper flakes (½ tsp)

Salt

Pepper

PREPARATION

1 WEEK BEFORE

★ Make **Ginger Beef Bone Broth** (single batch); freeze in 500ml/16fl oz portions. RECIPE PAGE 166

★ Make **Red Pepper Chickpea Soup** (double batch); freeze in 500ml/16fl oz portions. RECIPE PAGE 138

★ Eliminate processed foods and sugar from your diet and focus on whole foods.

2 DAYS BEFORE

★ Make **Peach Soup with Basil** (single batch); refrigerate in 500ml/16fl oz portions. RECIPE PAGE 70

★ Make **Carrot & Fennel Soup** (double batch); refrigerate in 500ml/16fl oz portions. RECIPE PAGE 146

★ Transfer Ginger Beef Bone Broth and Red Pepper Chickpea Soup from freezer to fridge to thaw.

★ Eliminate poultry, meat, and dairy from your diet.

★ Focus on vegetable-based meals supplemented with fish, grains, and legumes.

1 DAY BEFORE

★ Make **Avocado & Rocket Soup** (double batch); refrigerate in 500ml/16fl oz portions. RECIPE PAGE 29

★ Make **Strawberry Rhubarb Soup** (single batch); refrigerate in 250ml/9fl oz portions. RECIPE PAGE 54

★ Eliminate all animal products from your diet.

★ Eat vegetable-based meals with some legumes, grains, and nuts.

★ Drink at least 8 glasses of water.

DURING THE CLEANSE

DAILY SOUPS

BREAKFAST
Peach Soup with Basil (500ml/16fl oz)

SNACK
Ginger Beef Bone Broth (500ml/16fl oz)

LUNCH
Avocado & Rocket Soup (500ml/16fl oz)

SNACK
Carrot & Fennel Soup (500ml/16fl oz)

DINNER
Red Pepper Chickpea Soup (500ml/16fl oz)

DESSERT
Strawberry Rhubarb Soup (250ml/9fl oz)

ALTERNATIVES
Kiwi Kale Gazpacho (lunch)
RECIPE PAGE 36

Leafy Greens Detox Soup (dinner)
RECIPE PAGE 116

CLEANSE BOOSTERS

★ Drink 2 glasses of alkalized water between meals.

★ Perform 30–60 minutes of light to moderate exercise daily during cleanse, particularly hot yoga to aid in detoxification.

★ You may choose to receive a colonic treatment halfway through or at the end of your cleanse if you find them helpful.

Celery contains vitamin C, which has excellent antioxidant properties.

The lentils in this soup are high in fibre and rich in copper, which is important for bone strength and tissue health.

FRENCH LENTIL SOUP

Simple but immensely satisfying, this recipe allows the ingredients to shine. **Earthy lentils, sweet carrots,** and **savoury leeks** combine in a **rustic soup** that's hearty and filling. Serve hot.

 PREP & COOK
40 minutes

 QUANTITY
Makes 1 litre (1¾ pints)
Serving size 500ml (16fl oz)

 STORAGE
Refrigerated 5 days
Frozen 8 weeks

INGREDIENTS

1 tbsp olive oil

115g (4oz) leeks, rinsed
and diced

150g (5½oz) carrot, peeled
and diced

225g (8oz) celery, diced

200g (7oz) French green
lentils, uncooked

1.5 litres (2¾ pints) water

¼ tsp salt

⅛ tsp pepper

METHOD

1 In a medium casserole, heat olive oil over medium heat for 2 minutes. Add leeks, carrots, celery, and garlic and cook until leeks are translucent, about 5 minutes.

2 Add lentils and water, increase heat, and bring to the boil. Reduce heat, cover, and simmer for 20 minutes, or until lentils are fully cooked. Season with salt and pepper.

NUTRITION PER SERVING

calories	420
total fat	3g
cholesterol	0mg
sodium	390mg
carbohydrate	77g
dietary fibre	14g
sugars	7g
protein	26g

For an added...
health boost, use beef bone
broth instead of water and
finish with a touch of fresh
grated turmeric.

GRAPEFRUIT & FENNEL SOUP

This **refreshing, herbaceous blend** features the **tart, tangy flavour** of grapefruit along with **lightly sweet, earthy fennel.** Spinach adds a **vegetal note** as well as **antioxidant benefits.** Serve chilled.

 PREP & COOK
15 minutes

 QUANTITY
Makes 1 litre (1¾ pints)
Serving size 500ml (16fl oz)

 STORAGE
Refrigerated 5 days
Frozen 8 weeks

INGREDIENTS

500ml (16fl oz) fresh-squeezed grapefruit juice (about 6 grapefruits)

250ml (9fl oz) coconut water

100g (3½oz) fennel, bulb and fronds, chopped

85g (3oz) baby spinach

2 tsp agave nectar

METHOD

1 In a blender, combine grapefruit juice, coconut water, fennel, spinach, and agave nectar. Purée until mixture is smooth and fennel is completely incorporated.

2 If desired, transfer blending vessel to fridge to chill for 30 minutes. Blend briefly to recombine ingredients before serving.

NUTRITION PER SERVING

calories	192
total fat	2g
cholesterol	0mg
sodium	162mg
carbohydrate	40g
dietary fibre	6g
sugars	8g
protein	4g

If you find...
grapefruit juice too bitter, use orange juice instead. Oranges have similar health benefits with just a slightly higher sugar content.

Grapefruit is rich in
vitamin C and lycopene, a
compound with powerful
antioxidant properties.

LEAFY GREENS DETOX SOUP

Carrot, onion, and celery soften the bitterness of **kale and spinach** in this **verdant, detoxifying medley.** The hearty greens are **brightened by lemon juice** and a dash of red pepper flakes. Serve hot.

 PREP & COOK
40 minutes

 QUANTITY
Makes 1 litre (1¾ pints)
Serving size 500ml (16fl oz)

 STORAGE
Refrigerated 5 days
Frozen 8 weeks

INGREDIENTS

2 tbsp coconut oil

225g (8oz) onion, diced

225g (8oz) carrot, peeled and diced

150g (5½oz) celery, diced

2 tsp garlic, crushed (about 2 cloves)

1.2 litres (2 pints) water

140g (5oz) kale, stems removed and roughly chopped

350g (12oz) baby spinach

½ tsp red pepper flakes

2 tbsp lemon juice

½ tsp salt

METHOD

1 In a medium casserole, heat coconut oil over medium heat for 2 minutes. Add onion, carrot, celery, and garlic and cook until onion is translucent, about 5 minutes.

2 Add water, increase heat, and bring to the boil. Then reduce heat and simmer for 20 minutes, or until vegetables are cooked through. Remove from heat. Stir in kale, spinach, red pepper flakes, lemon juice, and salt.

3 Transfer contents of pot to blender and carefully purée until smooth and well combined. Add water if needed to thin.

For a heartier soup...
add 60g (2oz) cooked quinoa or 100g (3½oz) white beans before blending.

NUTRITION PER SERVING

calories	146
total fat	2g
cholesterol	0mg
sodium	476mg
carbohydrate	30g
dietary fibre	8g
sugars	12g
protein	5g

The vitamins and minerals in dark, leafy greens improve blood flow, purify the blood, and boost immunity

Pears are high in fibre and rich in copper, which plays an important role in energy production.

PEAR SOUP WITH CINNAMON

The **subtle, sweet flavour of pear** shines when combined with **juicy apples** and highlighted by **spicy cinnamon** and **freshly grated nutmeg** in this **warm, comforting soup.** Serve hot.

 **PREP & COOK**
20 minutes

 **QUANTITY**
Makes 1 litre (1¾ pints)
Serving size 500ml (16fl oz)

 **STORAGE**
Refrigerated 4 days
Frozen 8 weeks

INGREDIENTS

4 pears, peeled and diced
2 apples, peeled and diced
2 cinnamon sticks
500ml (16fl oz) water
1 tbsp palm sugar
¼ tsp fresh nutmeg, grated

METHOD

1 In a medium casserole, combine pears, apples, cinnamon sticks, and water. Bring to the boil over high heat, and then reduce heat and simmer for 10 minutes, or until fruit is cooked through.

2 Remove cinnamon sticks and transfer contents of pot to blender. Add sugar and grated nutmeg. Purée until smooth. Taste and adjust sugar based on sweetness of fruit.

NUTRITION PER SERVING	
calories	266
total fat	1g
cholesterol	0mg
sodium	3mg
carbohydrate	70g
dietary fibre	12g
sugars	48g
protein	2g

To make...
Creamy Vanilla Pear Soup,
swirl in 75g (2½oz) vanilla
Greek yogurt before
serving.

SPICY LEMONGRASS SOUP

This **soothing, aromatic soup** contains **lemongrass and ginger** to aid in digestion and pak choi to **reduce inflammation.** Chilli paste adds a **spicy note** as well as a **metabolic boost.** Serve hot.

 PREP & COOK
40 minutes

 QUANTITY
Makes 1 litre (1¾ pints)
Serving size 500ml (16fl oz)

 STORAGE
Refrigerated 5 days
Frozen 8 weeks

INGREDIENTS

¾ tbsp coconut oil

150g (5½oz) onion, diced

2 stalks lemongrass, cut into 5cm (2-inch) pieces

1½ tsp garlic, crushed

115g (4oz) carrot, peeled and cut into rounds

1 x 12.5-cm (5-inch) piece fresh ginger, peeled and cut into chunks

1 tbsp chilli paste

1.2 litres (2 pints) water

140g (5oz) pak choi, roughly chopped

2 tbsp spring onions, sliced

2 tbsp coriander, stalks removed and finely chopped

Juice of 1 lime

½ tsp salt

METHOD

1 In a medium casserole, heat coconut oil over medium heat for 2 minutes. Add onion, lemongrass, garlic, carrot, and ginger. Cook for 5 minutes, or until onion is translucent and garlic is fragrant.

2 Add chilli paste and continue to cook for another 2 minutes, stirring to combine.

3 Add water, increase heat, and bring to the boil. Then reduce heat, cover, and simmer for 20 minutes.

4 With a sieve or slotted spoon, remove lemongrass and ginger. Add pak choi and simmer for 3 minutes, or until it is cooked through.

5 Remove from heat. Stir in spring onions, coriander, lime juice, and salt.

NUTRITION PER SERVING

calories	121	carbohydrate	24g
total fat	2g	dietary fibre	7g
cholestoral	0g	sugars	8g
sodium	112mg	protein	5g

SPLIT PEA SOUP WITH KALE

Creamy and **packed with nutrition,** this hearty pea soup **flecked with kale** makes a satisfying meal on a chilly day. **Full of protein** and fibre, it's **comfort food** at its best. Serve hot.

 PREP & COOK
40 minutes

 QUANTITY
Makes 1 litre (1¾ pints)
Serving size 500ml (16fl oz)

 STORAGE
Refrigerated 4 days
Frozen 8 weeks

INGREDIENTS

¾ tbsp olive oil

75g (2½oz) carrot, peeled and diced

50g (1¾oz) celery, diced

75g (2½oz) onion, diced

1 tbsp garlic, crushed (about 3 cloves)

1.2 litres (2 pints) water

200g (7oz) split peas (uncooked)

30g (1oz) kale, deveined and finely chopped

1 tsp salt

⅛ tsp pepper

METHOD

1 In a medium casserole, heat olive oil over medium heat for 2 minutes. Add carrot, celery, onion, and garlic. Cook for 5 minutes, or until onion is translucent.

2 Add water and split peas, increase heat, and bring to the boil. Reduce heat, cover, and simmer for 25 minutes, or until peas have completely softened.

3 Stir in kale and cook until wilted, about 3 minutes. Season with salt and pepper. If desired, use an immersion blender to purée to a smooth consistency.

NUTRITION PER SERVING

calories	184
total fat	4g
cholesterol	0mg
sodium	1,428mg
carbohydrate	30g
dietary fibre	10g
sugars	6g
protein	10g

5
WINTER SOUPING

Winter souping features a detoxifying cleanse as well as an immunity-boosting cleanse that will help stave off winter's bite. Root vegetables are the stars in these heartier recipes that not only nourish but also help to energize the body during cold winter months.

Mushrooms are one of
the few food sources of
vitamin D, and the
only vegan source.

MUSHROOM & FREEKEH SOUP

High in protein with a **creamy texture**, this hearty combination of mushrooms, parsley, rosemary, and the **supergrain freekeh** is a rich, **satisfying** source of energy. Serve hot.

PREP & COOK
55 minutes

QUANTITY
Makes 1 litre (1¾ pints)
Serving size 500ml (16fl oz)

STORAGE
Refrigerated 5 days
Frozen 8 weeks

INGREDIENTS

2 tbsp olive oil

115g (4oz) leeks, rinsed and diced

75g (2½ oz) carrot, peeled and diced

50g (1¾oz) celery, diced

¾ tbsp garlic, crushed

½ tbsp tomato purée

50g (1¾oz) shiitake mushroom, diced

50g (1¾oz) chestnut mushroom, diced

750ml (1¼ pints) water

150g (5½oz) freekeh, cooked

2 tbsp parsley, finely chopped

½ tsp fresh rosemary, finely chopped

½ tsp salt

¼ tsp pepper

METHOD

1 In a medium casserole, heat olive oil over medium heat for 2 minutes. Add leeks, carrot, celery, and garlic, and cook until leeks are translucent, about 5 minutes.

2 Add tomato purée and continue to cook vegetables for another 5 minutes. Add mushrooms and water. Increase heat and bring to the boil, and then reduce heat and simmer for 10 minutes, or until mushrooms are cooked through.

3 Transfer contents of pot to blender and add freekeh. Blend until smooth, adding water to thin if needed. Add parsley, rosemary, salt, and pepper and blend briefly to combine.

NUTRITION PER SERVING	
calories	225
total fat	15g
cholesterol	0mg
sodium	648mg
carbohydrate	21g
dietary fibre	6g
sugars	4g
protein	5g

FIG & CARDAMOM SOUP

The **sweet flavour of dried figs** and **rich nuttiness of cashews** are accented with **floral notes of cardamom** in this protein-rich soup. It's a **satisfying morning meal** or energizing afternoon snack. Serve chilled.

 PREP & COOK
45 minutes

 QUANTITY
Makes 750ml (1 pint)
Serving size 250ml (9fl oz)

STORAGE
Refrigerated 5 days
Frozen 8 weeks

INGREDIENTS

500ml (16fl oz) water
150g (5½ oz) unsalted cashews
185g (6¼oz) cooked quinoa
½ tsp cardamom seeds (from 8–10 pods)
Seeds of 1 vanilla pod
1 tsp agave nectar
¼ cup dried figs, stalks removed and quartered

METHOD

1 In a small saucepan, heat water until just boiling. Place cashews in a medium, heat-safe bowl and add boiling water to cover. Leave to sit for 10 minutes.

2 Transfer cashews and soaking water to a blender. Purée for 30 seconds, or until smooth.

3 Using a mortar and pestle, grind cardamom seeds to a fine powder. Add quinoa, ground cardamom seeds, vanilla pod seeds, agave nectar, and dried figs to blender with processed cashews. Purée until smooth.

4 Transfer blending vessel to fridge to chill for 30 minutes. Blend briefly to recombine ingredients before serving. Add water or cashew milk to thin, if needed.

NUTRITION PER SERVING

calories	335
total fat	19g
cholesterol	0mg
sodium	3mg
carbohydrate	39g
dietary fibre	5g
sugars	9g
protein	11g

If you are...
unable to find cardamom, or feel the flavour is too intense, use a more subtle spice, like ginger, instead.

Heart-healthy figs are loaded with fibre and potassium, which helps regulate blood pressure.

Courgettes are a good source of potassium, which helps maintain normal blood pressure and healthy kidneys.

FENNEL & COURGETTE SOUP

Courgettes bring a **velvety texture** and mild flavour to this **delicate soup,** allowing the **aniseed notes of fennel** to shine. Onion and garlic provide a **savoury balance** and depth of flavour. Serve hot.

 PREP & COOK
20 minutes

 QUANTITY
Makes 1 litre (1¾ pints)
Serving size 500ml (16fl oz)

 STORAGE
Refrigerated 5 days
Frozen 8 weeks

INGREDIENTS

1 tbsp coconut oil

150g (5½oz) onion, diced

250g (9oz) fennel, bulb and fronds, diced

¾ tsp garlic, crushed

350g (12oz) courgettes, diced

1 litre (1¾ pints) water

⅛ tsp salt

⅛ tsp pepper

METHOD

1 In a medium casserole, heat coconut oil over medium heat for 2 minutes. Add onion, fennel, and garlic and cook until onion is translucent, about 5 minutes.

2 Add courgettes and water. Increase heat and bring to the boil, then reduce and simmer for 7 minutes, or until vegetables are cooked through. Remove from heat.

3 Transfer contents of pot to blender. Season with salt and pepper and purée until smooth.

NUTRITION PER SERVING

calories	113
total fat	2g
cholesterol	0mg
sodium	222mg
carbohydrate	22g
dietary fibre	7g
sugars	12g
protein	5g

To make...
Sweet Fennel & Pear Soup, omit garlic, salt, and pepper, and replace the courgettes with 175g (6oz) chopped and peeled pear.

WINTER ROOT VEGETABLE SOUP

This **smooth and creamy** combination highlights **hearty, vitamin-rich root vegetables** accented with **fresh thyme**. Warm and satisfying, it's delicious on a cold winter night. Serve hot.

 PREP & COOK
35 minutes

 QUANTITY
Makes 2.4 litre (4¹/₄ pints)
Serving size 500ml (16fl oz)

 STORAGE
Refrigerated 5 days
Frozen 8 weeks

INGREDIENTS

3 tbsp coconut oil

450g (1lb) onion, diced

2 tbsp garlic, crushed

175g (6oz) sweet potato,
  peeled and diced

125g (4½oz) butternut
  squash, peeled and diced

150g (5½oz) carrot, peeled
  and diced

150g (5½oz) parsnip,
  peeled and diced

150g (5½oz) celeriac,
  peeled and diced

2 litres (3½ pints) water

1 tsp fresh thyme, finely
  chopped

1 tsp salt

½ tsp pepper

METHOD

1 In a large casserole, heat coconut oil over medium heat for 2 minutes. Add onion and garlic and cook until onion is translucent, about 5 minutes.

2 Add sweet potato, butternut squash, carrot, parsnip, celeriac, and water. Increase heat and bring to the boil, then reduce heat and simmer for 10 minutes, or until vegetables are cooked through. Remove from heat.

3 Transfer contents of pot to blender and add thyme. Carefully purée until smooth and well combined. Season with salt and pepper.

NUTRITION PER SERVING	
calories	178
total fat	4g
cholesterol	0mg
sodium	538mg
carbohydrate	36g
dietary fibre	8g
sugars	12g
protein	4g

DETOXIFY
5-DAY CLEANSE

It's difficult to control your exposure to harmful environmental toxins, but you can work to combat them through dietary changes. These soups contain ingredients with detoxifying properties that work to cleanse the liver, purify the blood, and neutralize damaging compounds.

Follow for 5 days for optimal results. Incorporate a 1-day cleanse on a weekly basis for maintenance.

Shopping List

Fridge/Freezer
Beetroots (6 medium)
Onions (12)
Red onion (1)
Carrots (11 medium)
Courgette (6 medium)
Celery (16 stalks)
Garlic (23 cloves)
Baby spinach (2kg/4½lb)
Kale (400g/14oz, chopped)
Fennel (4 large bulbs)
Broccoli, florets (2kg/4½lb)
Parsnips (5 medium)
Rocket (500g/1lb 2oz)
Fresh ginger (1 [7.5cm/3-inch] piece)
Granny Smith apples (6 large)
Lemons (4)
Orange juice, fresh squeezed (750ml/1¼ pints)
Fresh basil (90g/3¼oz, chopped)
Fresh mint (90g/3¼oz, chopped)

Store cupboard
Olive oil (3 tbsp)
Coconut oil (250ml/9fl oz + 1 tbsp)
Artichoke hearts (3 x 400g cans)
Water (14 litres/3 gallons)
Vanilla essence (1½ tbsp)
Cinnamon sticks (2)
Red pepper flakes (1½ tsp)
Salt
Pepper

PREPARATION			DURING THE CLEANSE	
1 WEEK BEFORE	**2 DAYS BEFORE**	**1 DAY BEFORE**	**DAILY SOUPS**	**CLEANSE BOOSTERS**
★ Make **Broccoli Rocket Soup** (triple batch); freeze in 500ml/16fl oz portions. RECIPE PAGE 143	★ Make **Fennel & Courgette Soup** (triple batch); refrigerate in 500ml/16fl oz portions. RECIPE PAGE 129	★ Make **Beetroot & Orange Soup** (triple batch); refrigerate in 500ml/16fl oz portions. RECIPE PAGE 40	**BREAKFAST** Beetroot & Orange Soup (500ml/16fl oz)	★ Drink 8 glasses of alkalized water between meals.
★ Make **Artichoke Basil Soup** (triple batch); freeze in 500ml/16fl oz portions. RECIPE PAGE 75	★ Make **Leafy Greens Detox Soup** (triple batch); refrigerate in 500ml/16fl oz portions. RECIPE PAGE 116	★ Make **Apple & Parsnip Soup** (double batch); refrigerate in 500ml/16fl oz portions. RECIPE PAGE 106	**SNACK** Broccoli Rocket Soup (500ml/16fl oz) **LUNCH** Fennel & Courgette Soup (500ml/16fl oz)	★ Perform 30–60 minutes of light to moderate exercise daily during cleanse, particularly hot yoga or cardio, to aid in detoxification.
★ Eliminate processed foods and sugar from your diet and focus on whole foods.	★ Eliminate poultry, meat, and dairy from your diet.	★ Transfer Broccoli Rocket Soup and Artichoke Basil Soup from freezer to fridge to thaw.	**SNACK** Leafy Greens Detox Soup (500ml/16fl oz) **DINNER** Artichoke Basil Soup (500ml/16fl oz)	★ You may choose to receive a colonic treatment halfway through or at the end of your cleanse if you find them helpful.
	★ Focus on vegetable-based meals supplemented with fish, grains, and legumes.	★ Eliminate all animal products from your diet.	**DESSERT** Apple & Parsnip Soup (250ml/9fl oz)	
		★ Eat vegetable-based meals with some legumes, grains, and nuts.	**ALTERNATIVES** Strawberry Chia Soup (breakfast) RECIPE PAGE 45 Red Pepper Chickpea Soup (dinner) RECIPE PAGE 138	
		★ Drink at least 8 glasses of water.		

ANCIENT GRAINS SOUP

The **ancient grains** amaranth, freekeh, and quinoa bring a **robust texture** and **earthy flavour** to this rich tomato soup. With a **savoury mix** of vegetables, it's **nutritious and satisfying**. Serve hot.

 PREP & COOK
45 minutes

 QUANTITY
1 litre (1¾ pints)
Serving size 500ml (16fl oz)

 STORAGE
Refrigerated 5 days
Frozen 8 weeks

INGREDIENTS

¾ tbsp olive oil

75g (2½oz) onion, diced

50g (1¾ oz) celery, diced

75g (2½oz) carrot, peeled and diced

2 tsp garlic, crushed (about 2 cloves)

400g can chopped tomatoes

60g (2oz) amaranth, cooked

45g (1½ oz) freekeh, cooked

45g (1½ oz) quinoa, cooked

400ml (14fl oz) water

1 tsp parsley, chopped

¼ tsp salt

¼ tsp pepper

METHOD

1 In a medium casserole, heat olive oil over medium heat for 2 minutes. Add onion, celery, carrot, and garlic, and cook until onion is translucent, about 5 minutes.

2 Add tomatoes (with juices), amaranth, freekeh, quinoa, and water. Increase heat and bring to the boil, and then reduce heat and simmer for 15 minutes. Remove from heat.

3 Transfer contents of pot to blender and add parsley. Purée until well combined. Season with salt and pepper.

NUTRITION PER SERVING

calories	220
total fat	7g
cholesterol	0mg
sodium	692mg
carbohydrate	34g
dietary fibre	6g
sugars	9g
protein	6g

ROASTED ARTICHOKE SOUP

Jerusalem artichokes, also called sunchokes, are a small tuber with a **delicate, slightly sweet flavour.** Roasted alongside **cauliflower,** they yield an **earthy, nutty soup** with a velvety texture. Serve hot.

 PREP & COOK
35 minutes

 QUANTITY
Makes 1.5 litres (2¾ pints)
Serving size 500ml (16fl oz)

 STORAGE
Refrigerated 5 days
Frozen 8 weeks

INGREDIENTS

175g (6oz) cauliflower florets

225g (8oz) onion, diced

25g (scant 1oz) celery, diced

6 Jerusalem artichokes, sliced

2 tbsp olive oil

Juice of ½ lemon

1.2 litres (2 pints) water

3 tbsp parsley, finely chopped

¼ tsp cayenne

½ tsp salt

¼ tsp pepper

METHOD

1 Preheat oven to 230°C (450°F/Gas 8). Line a baking tray with foil.

2 In a medium bowl, combine cauliflower, onion, celery, and artichokes. Drizzle with olive oil and toss to coat. Spread vegetables on prepared baking tray and bake for 20 minutes, or until they begin to brown.

3 In a blender, combine roasted vegetables, lemon juice, water, parsley, and cayenne. Blend until smooth, adding water if needed to thin. Season with salt and pepper and blend briefly to combine.

NUTRITION PER SERVING

calories	209
total fat	9g
cholesterol	0mg
sodium	423mg
carbohydrate	13g
dietary fibre	5g
sugars	15g
protein	4g

Try using...
225g (8oz) parsnips, peeled and diced, if Jerusalem artichokes are unavailable.

SPICED CHICKPEA SOUP

This soup features the **spicy, exotic flavours** of cinnamon, cumin, and paprika, along with **hearty chickpeas**. With plenty of protein, it's a **warm and satisfying** meal. Serve hot.

 PREP & COOK
35 minutes

 QUANTITY
Makes 1 litre (1¾ pints)
Serving size 500ml (16fl oz)

 STORAGE
Refrigerated 5 days
Frozen 8 weeks

INGREDIENTS

1½ tbsp olive oil

150g (5½oz) onion, diced

1 tbsp garlic, crushed
(about 3 cloves)

1 tsp cumin

2 tsp cinnamon

¼ tsp cayenne

½ tsp paprika

225g can chopped tomato

400g can chickpeas, drained
and rinsed

1 litre (1¾ pints) water

85g (3oz) baby spinach

1 tbsp coriander, chopped

¼ tsp salt

METHOD

1 In a medium casserole, heat olive oil over medium heat for 2 minutes. Add onion and garlic and cook until onion is translucent, about 5 minutes. Add cumin, cinnamon, cayenne, paprika, and tomatoes and cook for another 3 minutes.

2 Add chickpeas and water. Increase heat and bring to the boil, then reduce heat, cover, and simmer for 15 minutes. Remove from heat.

3 Transfer contents of pot to blender. Add spinach and coriander to blender and blend until well combined. Add water to thin if needed. Season with salt and blend briefly to combine.

NUTRITION PER SERVING

calories	296	carbohydrate	54g
total fat	6g	dietary fibre	17g
cholesterol	0mg	sugars	14g
sodium	565mg	protein	13g

RED PEPPER CHICKPEA SOUP

This **vibrant soup** brings together the flavours of **roasted red peppers** and **nutty chickpeas** in one creamy, satisfying bowl. Fire-roasted tomatoes add a **savoury, slightly smoky** note. Serve hot.

 **PREP & COOK**
30 minutes

 QUANTITY
Makes 1 litre (1¾ pints)
Serving size 500ml (16fl oz)

 STORAGE
Refrigerated 5 days
Frozen 8 weeks

INGREDIENTS

1½ tbsp olive oil

225g (8oz) onion, diced

2 tbsp garlic, crushed (about 2 cloves)

115g (4oz) chargrilled tomatoes, skins removed, seeded and chopped

250g (9oz) roasted red pepper, rinsed and drained

125g can chickpeas, rinsed and drained

1 litre (1¾ pints) water

2 tbsp parsley, finely chopped

¼ tsp salt

METHOD

1 In a medium casserole, heat olive oil over medium heat for 2 minutes. Add onion and garlic and cook until onion is translucent, about 5 minutes.

2 Add diced tomatoes, roasted red pepper, chickpeas, and water. Increase heat and bring to the boil, then reduce heat and cover. Simmer for 10 minutes. Remove from heat.

3 Transfer contents of pot to blender and purée until smooth. Add parsley and salt, and blend briefly to combine.

To boost...
the health benefits of this soup, use chicken bone broth in place of water and add 1 tsp red pepper flakes with the diced tomatoes.

NUTRITION PER SERVING

calories	280
total fat	5g
cholesterol	0mg
sodium	317mg
carbohydrate	54g
dietary fibre	11g
sugars	16g
protein	14g

Red pepper is an excellent source of antioxidants and has more vitamin C per serving than an orange.

CHAI SPICED ALMOND SOUP

With **star anise, cinnamon, ginger,** and **cardamom,** this soup tastes like a spicy, dairy-free version of your **favourite chai latte.** Almonds add a **creamy texture** as well as **nourishing protein.** Serve chilled.

 PREP & COOK
12 hours

 QUANTITY
Makes 1 litre (1¾ pints)
Serving size 250ml (9fl oz)

 STORAGE
Refrigerated 5 days
Frozen 8 weeks

INGREDIENTS

2 tbsp decaffeinated loose-leaf black tea, or
2 decaffeinated black tea bags

1 litre (1¾ pints) water

150g (5½oz) raw almonds

2 cinnamon sticks

1 star anise

4 tbsp agave nectar

2 tsp vanilla, or seeds from 1 vanilla pod

1½ tbsp fresh ginger, grated

¾ tsp ground cardamom

½ tsp cracked black pepper

½ tsp cinnamon

METHOD

1 Place tea in a 1-litre (1¾-pint) heat-resistant jar. In a saucepan or kettle, bring water to the boil over high heat. Pour boiling water over tea. Steep for 4–5 minutes. Strain and discard tea leaves.

2 Add almonds, cinnamon sticks, and star anise to tea. Cool and refrigerate overnight.

3 Remove cinnamon sticks and star anise from tea. Transfer contents of jar to blender and add agave nectar, vanilla, ginger, cardamom, black pepper, and cinnamon. Blend until smooth.

NUTRITION PER SERVING	
calories	287
total fat	18g
cholesterol	0mg
sodium	6mg
carbohydrate	26g
dietary fibre	5g
sugars	16g
protein	8g

For a sweet,... earthy flavour, try rooibos tea instead of black tea.

MUSHROOM & MILLET SOUP

This soup features the **ancient grain millet**, which is rich in fibre and protein as well as vitamin B3. Paired with **savoury, earthy mushrooms**, it makes for a **satisfying yet low-calorie** meal. Serve hot.

 **PREP & COOK**
35 minutes

 QUANTITY
Makes 1 litre (1¾ pints)
Serving size 500ml (16fl oz)

 STORAGE
Refrigerated 5 days
Frozen 8 weeks

INGREDIENTS

1 tbsp olive oil

150g (5½ oz) onion, diced

1 tbsp garlic, crushed
(about 3 cloves)

400g (14oz) chestnuts
mushrooms, diced

750ml (1¼ pints) water

¼ cup millet, cooked

Juice of ½ lemon

2 tbsp parsley, finely
chopped

½ tsp fresh thyme, finely
chopped

¾ tsp salt

¼ tsp pepper

½ tsp truffle oil (optional)

METHOD

1 In a medium casserole, heat olive oil over medium heat for 2 minutes. Add onion and garlic and cook until onion is translucent, about 5 minutes.

2 Add mushrooms and water. Increase heat and bring to the boil, then reduce heat and simmer for 10 minutes, or until mushrooms are cooked through. Remove from heat.

3 Transfer contents of pot to blender, and add millet, lemon juice, parsley, and thyme. Purée until smooth. Season with salt and pepper, and add truffle oil, if using. Blend briefly to combine.

NUTRITION PER SERVING

calories	115	carbohydrate	22g
total fat	2g	dietary fibre	3g
cholesterol	0mg	sugars	7g
sodium	885mg	protein	6g

Broccoli is a significant source of vitamin K, which aids in keeping bones and blood healthy.

BROCCOLI ROCKET SOUP

Hearty broccoli and **peppery rocket** come together in this **light-bodied soup** that is both **energizing and detoxifying.** A squeeze of lemon adds **brightness and zest.** Serve hot.

 PREP & COOK
20 minutes

 QUANTITY
Makes 1 litre (1¾ pints)
Serving size 500ml (16fl oz)

 STORAGE
Refrigerated 5 days
Frozen 8 weeks

INGREDIENTS

1 tbsp coconut oil

150g (5½oz) onion, diced

2 tsp garlic, crushed (about 2 cloves)

675g (1½lb) broccoli florets

850ml (1½ pints) water

175g (6oz) baby rocket, tightly packed

¼ tsp salt

⅛ tsp pepper

1 wedge lemon

METHOD

1 In a medium casserole, heat coconut oil over medium heat for 2 minutes. Add onion and garlic, and cook until onion is translucent, about 5 minutes.

2 Add broccoli and water to pot. Increase heat and bring to the boil, then reduce heat, cover, and simmer for 5 minutes, or until broccoli is cooked through. Remove from heat.

3 Transfer contents of pot to blender and add rocket. Blend until smooth and well combined. Season with salt and pepper and finish with a squeeze of lemon.

NUTRITION PER SERVING

calories	117
total fat	2g
cholesterol	0mg
sodium	69mg
carbohydrate	22g
dietary fibre	7g
sugars	7g
protein	7g

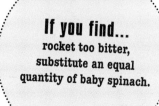

If you find...
rocket too bitter,
substitute an equal
quantity of baby spinach.

IMMUNE BOOST
3-DAY CLEANSE

Your immune system monitors and protects against disease and infection on a daily basis. Poor diet and lifestyle choices can negatively affect your immune system, and a weakened immune system can leave your body susceptible to dysfunctions and more serious infections.

Follow for 3 days to strengthen immunity.

shopping List

Fridge/Freezer
Onions (6)
Celery (4 stalks)
Carrots (11 medium)
Garlic (19 cloves)
Fennel (3 bulbs)
Strawberries (900g/2lb)
Bananas (4)
Parsley (1 bunch)
Fresh dill (3 tbsp, finely chopped)
Ginger (½ tsp, grated)
Bone-in chicken pieces (1kg/2 lb)
Chicken feet (1kg/2 lb)

Pantry
Olive oil (9 tbsp)
Coconut oil (1^1/$_2$ tbsp)
Apple cider vinegar (2 tbsp)
Red wine vinegar (4 tsp)
Water (9 litres/16 pints)
Coconut water (1 litre/1¾ pints)
Light coconut milk (120ml/4fl oz)
Chargrilled tomatoes, skins removed, seeeded and chopped (400g/14oz)
Chopped tomatoes (2 x 400g cans)
Roasted red peppers (1kg/2¼lb)
Linseed, ground (4 tsp)
Chia seeds (4 tsp)
Walnuts (200g/7oz)
Almonds, blanched (150g/5½oz)
Agave nectar (3 tsp)
Bay leaf (1)
Red pepper flakes (½ tsp)
Cayenne (1 tsp)
Curry powder (2 tbsp)
Cinnamon sticks (2)
Salt
pepper

PREPARATION			DURING THE CLEANSE	
1 WEEK BEFORE	**2 DAYS BEFORE**	**1 DAY BEFORE**	**DAILY SOUPS**	**CLEANSE BOOSTERS**
★ Make **Jalapeño Chicken Broth** (single batch); freeze in 500ml/16fl oz portions. RECIPE PAGE 156	★ Make **Curried Carrot Soup** (double batch); refrigerate in 500ml/16fl oz portions. RECIPE PAGE 38	★ Make **Strawberry Chia Soup** (double batch); refrigerate in 500ml/16fl oz portions. RECIPE PAGE 45	**BREAKFAST** Strawberry Chia Soup (500ml/16fl oz)	★ Drink 2 glasses of alkalized water between meals.
★ Make **Red Pepper Romesco Soup** (double batch); freeze in 500ml/16fl oz portions. RECIPE PAGE 63	★ Make **Tomato Broth with Dill** (single batch); refrigerate in 500ml/16fl oz portions. RECIPE PAGE 173	★ **Banana Walnut Soup** (double batch); refrigerate in 250ml/9fl oz portions. RECIPE PAGE 107	**SNACK** Jalapeño Chicken Broth (500ml/16fl oz)	★ Perform 30–60 minutes of light to moderate exercise daily during cleanse.
★ Eliminate processed foods and sugar from your diet and focus on whole foods.	★ Eliminate poultry, meat, and dairy from your diet.	★ Transfer Jalapeño Chicken Broth and Red Pepper Romesco Soup from freezer to fridge to thaw.	**LUNCH** Red Pepper Romesco Soup (500ml/16fl oz)	
	★ Focus on vegetable-based meals supplemented with fish, grains, and legumes.	★ Eat vegetable-based meals with some legumes, grains, and nuts.	**SNACK** Curried Carrot Soup (500ml/16fl oz)	
		★ Drink at least 8 glasses of water.	**DINNER** Tomato Broth with Dill (500ml/16fl oz)	
			DESSERT Banana Walnut Soup (250ml/9fl oz)	
			ALTERNATIVES Citrus Soup with Lavender (breakfast) RECIPE PAGE 150	
			Asparagus Soup with Mint (lunch) RECIPE PAGE 51	

CARROT & FENNEL SOUP

Roasting with **a touch of honey** brings out the **earthy sweetness** of **carrots and fennel,** which is complemented by savoury **fresh thyme** in this **creamy, comforting soup.** Serve hot.

 PREP & COOK
30 minutes

 QUANTITY
Makes 1 litre (1¾ pints)
Serving size 500ml (16fl oz)

 STORAGE
Refrigerated 5 days
Frozen 8 weeks

INGREDIENTS

300g (10oz) carrot, peeled and diced

175g (6oz) fennel, diced

150g (5½oz) onion, diced

2 tsbp coconut oil

2 tbsp honey

1 litre (1¾ pints) water

½ tsp fresh thyme, finely chopped

¼ tsp salt

¼ tsp pepper

METHOD

1 Preheat oven to 220°C (425°F/Gas 7). Line a baking tray with foil.

2 In a medium bowl, combine carrot, fennel, and onion. Drizzle with coconut oil and honey and toss to combine. Spread vegetables on prepared baking tray and roast for 12–15 minutes, or until they begin to caramelize.

3 In a blender, combine roasted vegetables, water, and thyme. Blend until smooth. Season with salt and pepper and heat before serving if needed.

NUTRITION PER SERVING

calories	293
total fat	14g
cholesterol	0mg
sodium	428mg
carbohydrate	43g
dietary fibre	8g
sugars	13g
protein	3g

To make...
Zesty Carrot Soup, add 140g (5oz) Greek yogurt to blender, replace thyme with 2 tbsp finely chopped coriander, add ½ tsp cumin, and finish with a squirt of lime juice.

Honey helps facilitate caramelization when roasting vegetables.

BUTTERNUT BLACK BEAN SOUP

Chunks of **sweet butternut squash** are complemented by a **smoky tomato broth** and **robust black beans** in this fibre-rich, filling soup. Chilli powder adds a hint of **warming spice.** Serve hot.

PREP & COOK
45 minutes

QUANTITY
Makes 1 litre (1¾ pints)
Serving size 500ml (16fl oz)

STORAGE
Refrigerated 5 days
Frozen 8 weeks

INGREDIENTS

2 tbsp olive oil

115g (4oz) onion, diced

2½ tbsp garlic, crushed (about 7 cloves)

1½ tsp tomato purée

100g (3½oz) chargrilled tomatoes, skins removed, seeded and chopped

600ml (1 pint) water

1½ tsp chilli powder

¾ tsp coriander

¾ tsp cumin

1 tsp chile de árbol or cayenne powder (optional)

125g (4½oz) butternut squash, peeled and cubed

85g can black beans, drained and rinsed

1½ tbsp coriander, finely chopped

Juice of 1 lime

¼ tsp salt

METHOD

1 In a medium casserole, heat olive oil over medium heat for 2 minutes. Add onion and garlic, and cook until onion is translucent, about 5 minutes. Stir in tomato purée and cook for another 3 minutes.

2 Add diced tomatoes, water, chilli powder, coriander, cumin, chile de árbol (if using), butternut squash, and black beans.

3 Increase heat and bring to the boil, then reduce heat, cover, and simmer until butternut squash is cooked through, about 20 minutes.

4 Before serving, stir in coriander and lime juice. Season with salt to taste.

NUTRITION PER SERVING

calories	232
total fat	4g
cholesterol	0mg
sodium	534mg
carbohydrate	43g
dietary fibre	13g
sugars	6g
protein	11g

CITRUS SOUP WITH LAVENDER

Bright citrus flavours of orange and grapefruit are combined with nutty chia and **soothing lavender** to create this **fresh, invigorating soup.** Enjoy for breakfast or dessert. Serve chilled.

 **PREP & COOK**
20 minutes

 QUANTITY
Makes 750ml (1¼ pints)
Serving size 250ml (9fl oz)

 STORAGE
Refrigerated 5 days
Frozen 8 weeks

INGREDIENTS

3 oranges

2 grapefruits

150ml (¼ pint) coconut water

2 tsp fresh lavender, finely chopped

2 tbsp chia seeds

METHOD

1 Supreme oranges and grapefruits by carefully slicing away the rinds and removing the membranes. Reserve the juice.

2 In a blender, combine orange supremes, grapefruit supremes, reserved citrus juice, coconut water, and lavender. Purée until smooth, about 30 seconds.

3 If desired, transfer blending vessel to fridge to chill for 30 minutes. Before serving, stir in chia seeds and leave to sit until chia seeds are plump, about 10 minutes.

NUTRITION PER SERVING	
calories	185
total fat	3g
cholesterol	0mg
sodium	15mg
carbohydrate	39g
dietary fibre	8g
sugars	25g
protein	4g

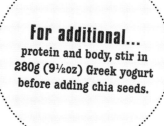

For additional...
protein and body, stir in 280g (9½oz) Greek yogurt before adding chia seeds.

Lavender has natural anti-inflammatory benefits and aids in digestion.

Flavonoids in citrus fruits can neutralize free radicals.

NUTMEG SWEET POTATO SOUP

This **cozy soup** tastes like the holidays, with the **warm spice of nutmeg,** hearty **sweet potatoes,** and a **touch of maple syrup.** Smooth and **creamy,** it's a delicious and healthy treat. Serve hot.

 PREP & COOK
45 minutes

 QUANTITY
Makes 1 litre (1¾ pints)
Serving size 500ml (16fl oz)

 STORAGE
Refrigerated 5 days
Frozen 8 weeks

INGREDIENTS

1½ tbsp coconut oil

115g (4oz) celery, diced

225g (8oz) onion, diced

1 tsp garlic, crushed (about 1 clove)

1 litre (1¾ pints) water

500g (1lb 2oz) sweet potato, peeled and cubed

4 tbsp pure maple syrup

½ tsp fresh nutmeg, grated

⅛ tsp salt

METHOD

1 In a medium casserole, heat coconut oil over medium heat for 2 minutes. Add celery, onion, and garlic. Cook until onion becomes translucent, about 5 minutes.

2 Add water and sweet potato. Increase heat and bring to the boil, then reduce heat to a simmer and cover. Simmer until sweet potatoes are cooked through, about 15 minutes. Remove from heat.

3 Add contents of pot to blender along with maple syrup and nutmeg. Blend until smooth. Season with salt and blend briefly to combine.

NUTRITION PER SERVING

calories	344
total fat	2g
cholesterol	0mg
sodium	285mg
carbohydrate	80g
dietary fibre	9g
sugars	38g
protein	5g

For a lighter flavour... use 375g (13oz) butternut squash (peeled and diced) instead of sweet potatoes.

The natural sugars in sweet potatoes release slowly, ensuring an extended source of energy.

Unlike most other sweeteners, pure maple syrup does not cause spikes in blood sugar.

6
BROTHS & CONSOMMÉS

Digestive health and anti-inflammatory cleanses, which utilize restorative broths and consommés, are featured here. The recipes in this part include both vegetable- and protein-based ingredients that are delicious on their own or as a base for other soups.

JALAPEÑO CHICKEN BROTH

Nourishing bone broth is a comforting snack on its own or a nutrient-rich **addition to soups.** This recipe for **basic chicken bone broth** includes the optional addition of **lime and jalapeños.** Serve hot.

 PREP & COOK
7–24 hours

 QUANTITY
Makes 1.5 litres (2¾ pints)
Serving size 500ml (16fl oz)

 STORAGE
Refrigerated 5 days
Frozen 8 weeks

INGREDIENTS

2 tbsp olive oil

1kg (2lb) bone-in chicken pieces (legs, backs, and necks)

1kg (2lb) chicken feet

3 litres (5¼ pints) water

2 tbsp apple cider vinegar

150g (5½oz) onion, chopped

200g (7oz) celery, chopped

150g (5½oz) carrot, chopped

8 garlic cloves, peeled

1 bay leaf

½ bunch parsley

2 tbsp jalapeño pepper, thinly sliced (optional)

Juice of 4 limes (optional)

½ tsp salt

½ tsp pepper

METHOD

1 In a large casserole, heat olive oil over medium heat for 2 minutes. Add chicken pieces and cook for 8 minutes, turning to brown on all sides.

2 Add water to cover chicken by 7.5–10cm (3–4 inches). Add apple cider vinegar and cook over medium-high heat until boiling, about 35 minutes.

3 Reduce heat to simmer and cover. Simmer for at least 6 hours and up to 24 hours. Skim broth intermittently, and add water as needed to ensure bones remain covered.

4 Two hours before removing broth from the stove, add onion, celery, carrot, garlic, bay leaf, and parsley. Cook for remaining 2 hours, and then remove pot from heat.

5 Strain broth, discarding solids. Add jalapeños and lime juice (if using), and salt and pepper. Transfer to fridge to cool. Once cool, skim fat from surface. Heat before serving.

NUTRITION PER SERVING

calories	68	carbohydrate	15g
total fat	3g	dietary fibre	1g
cholestoral	0mg	sugars	3g
sodium	404mg	protein	1g

The capsaicin in jalapeños is a powerful inflammation-fighting compound.

SESAME VEGETABLE BROTH

The **rich flavour of toasted sesame oil** is perfectly balanced with the bright background **notes of lime** in this Asian-inspired broth. **Ginger provides spice** and **promotes healthy digestion.** Serve hot.

 PREP & COOK
1 hour

 QUANTITY
Makes 1.5 litres (2¾ pints)
Serving size 500ml (16fl oz)

 STORAGE
Refrigerated 5 days
Frozen 8 weeks

INGREDIENTS

2 tbsp olive oil

150g (5½oz) onion, chopped

60g (2oz) lemongrass, roughly chopped

100g (3½oz) ginger, unpeeled and roughly chopped

150g (5½oz) carrot, chopped

5 garlic cloves, whole

2 litres (3½ pints) water

3 tbsp tamari

Juice of 3 limes

1 tsp toasted sesame oil

30g (1oz) spring onions, thinly sliced

METHOD

1 In a medium casserole, heat olive oil over medium heat for 2 minutes. Add onion, lemongrass, ginger, carrot, and garlic. Cook until onion is translucent, about 5 minutes.

2 Add water, increase heat, and bring to the boil. Reduce heat, cover, and simmer for 40 minutes. Remove from heat.

3 Strain broth and discard vegetables. Add tamari, lime juice, and sesame oil. Top with spring onions.

To make...
Light Vegetable Soup, add 165g (6oz) spinach, 50g (1¾oz) sliced mushrooms, 75g (2½oz) peeled carrot strips, and 30g (1oz) chopped coriander to the hot broth.

NUTRITION PER SERVING	
calories	76
total fat	4g
cholesterol	10mg
sodium	2,854mg
carbohydrate	7g
dietary fibre	0g
sugars	3g
protein	5g

This warming broth makes an excellent base for vegetable soups.

Citrusy lemongrass adds a boost of folate, folic acid, and other minerals.

CARROT CONSOMMÉ

The **mild citrus flavour** of lemongrass complements the natural **sweetness of carrots** in this **aromatic consommé.** An excellent source of vitamin C, it's an **immune-boosting** tonic against colds. Serve hot.

PREP & COOK
1 hour 10 minutes

QUANTITY
Makes 1.5 litres (2¾ pints)
Serving size 500ml (16fl oz)

STORAGE
Refrigerated 5 days
Frozen 8 weeks

INGREDIENTS

5 egg whites

450g (1lb) carrot, peeled and grated

85g (3oz) lemongrass, thinly sliced

50g (1¾oz) ginger, chopped

2 litres (3½ pints) fresh carrot juice, chilled

2 tbsp coriander, finely chopped

1 tsp lime zest

½ tsp salt

METHOD

1 In a small bowl, lightly beat egg whites. Add beaten egg whites to a medium casserole along with grated carrots, lemongrass, ginger, and carrot juice. Stir to combine.

2 Bring the mixture to a simmer over medium heat, stirring frequently. Within about 20 minutes a "raft" should form at the top. With a spoon, gently break a hole in the middle to allow the consommé to simmer.

3 Reduce heat to medium-low and continue to simmer for 30 minutes. Remove from heat.

4 Line a mesh sieve with muslin or a coffee filter, and place over a large bowl or pot. Gently ladle the consommé into strainer to remove vegetable solids.

5 Add coriander, lime zest, and salt to strained consommé. Warm before serving, if needed.

NUTRITION PER SERVING

calories	361
total fat	2g
cholesterol	0mg
sodium	983mg
carbohydrate	78g
dietary fibre	9g
sugars	31g
protein	14g

SHIITAKE GINGER BROTH

This **umami-rich broth** is earthy and satisfying. Shiitakes provide **B-complex vitamins** along with a **variety of minerals**. Ginger aids in digestion and has **anti-inflammatory benefits**. Serve hot.

 **PREP & COOK**
45 minutes

 QUANTITY
Makes 1.5 litres (2¾ pints)
Serving size 500ml (16fl oz)

 STORAGE
Refrigerated 5 days
Frozen 8 weeks

INGREDIENTS

1 tbsp olive oil

150g (5½ oz) onion, chopped

75g (2½ oz) carrot, peeled and chopped

100g (3½oz) fresh ginger, roughly chopped

1 (2.5cm/1-inch) piece fresh ginger, grated

5 garlic cloves, whole

100g (3½oz) shiitake mushrooms, quartered

5 stalks parsley

2 litres (3½ pints) water

4 tbsp tamari

METHOD

1 In a medium casserole, heat olive oil over medium heat for 2 minutes. Add onion, carrot, chopped ginger, and garlic. Cook until onion is translucent, about 5 minutes.

2 Add shiitake mushrooms, parsley, and water to pot. Increase heat and bring to boil, and then reduce heat, cover, and simmer for 30 minutes. Remove from heat.

3 Line a mesh sieve with muslin and strain broth, discarding vegetable solids. Stir in tamari and fresh grated ginger. Heat before serving if needed.

For a richer flavour...
and added health benefits, use beef bone broth instead of water.

NUTRITION PER SERVING

calories	144
total fat	2g
cholesterol	0mg
sodium	1,318mg
carbohydrate	30g
dietary fibre	5g
sugars	8g
protein	6g

DIGESTIVE HEALTH
5-DAY CLEANSE

Flatten your belly, ease pain and bloating, and aid digestion with this restorative cleanse. Processed foods, fried foods, acidic foods, and dairy can all contribute to digestive issues. This cleanse focuses on hydrating veggies and fibre-rich foods that work to cleanse, hydrate, and restore the digestive system.

Follow for 5 days.

Shopping List

Fridge/Freezer
Leeks (450g/1lb, diced)
Carrots (4 medium)
Celery (6 stalks)
Courgettes (3)
Garlic (33 cloves)
Onions (6)
Fennel (7 bulbs)
Butternut squash (1 medium)
Baby spinach (975g/2lb 3oz)
Raspberries (450g/1lb)
Lemon (1)
Limes (6)
Grapefruits (9)
Papaya (2kg/4lb, cubed)
Coriander (1 bunch)
Vanilla yogurt (280g/9½oz)

Store cupboard
Olive oil (120ml/4fl oz)
Coconut oil (3 tbsp)
French green lentils (2 cups)
Unsweetened coconut flakes (225g/8oz)
Water (10 litres/17½ pints)
Coconut water (1.9 litres/3¼ pints)
Hemp seeds (8 tbsp)
Tomato purée (4½ tsp)
Fire-roasted diced tomatoes (400g can)
Black beans (2 x [400g cans])
Agave nectar (2 tbsp)
Spirulina powder (4½ tsp)
Chilli powder (4½ tsp)
Ground coriander (2¼ tsp)
Ground cumin (2¼ tsp)
Salt
Pepper

PREPARATION

DURING THE CLEANSE

1 WEEK BEFORE	2 DAYS BEFORE	1 DAY BEFORE	DAILY SOUPS	CLEANSE BOOSTERS

★ Make **French Lentil Soup** (double batch); freeze in 500ml/16fl oz portions.
RECIPE PAGE 113

★ Make **Butternut Black Bean Soup** (triple batch); freeze in 500ml/16fl oz portions.
RECIPE PAGE 148

★ Eliminate processed foods and sugar from your diet and focus on whole foods.

★ Make **Fennel & Courgette Soup** (triple batch); refrigerate in 500ml/16fl oz portions.
RECIPE PAGE 129

★ Make **Grapefruit & Fennel Soup** (triple batch); refrigerate in 500ml/16fl oz portions.
RECIPE PAGE 114

★ Eliminate poultry, meat, and dairy from your diet.

★ Focus on vegetable-based meals supplemented with fish, grains, and legumes.

★ Make **Papaya & Spinach Soup** (triple batch); refrigerate in 500ml/16fl oz portions.
RECIPE PAGE 71

★ Make **Raspberry Coconut Soup** (double batch); refrigerate in 250ml/9fl oz portions.
RECIPE PAGE 87

★ Transfer French Lentil Soup and Butternut Black Bean Soup from freezer to fridge to thaw.

★ Eliminate all animal products from your diet.

★ Eat vegetable-based meals with some legumes, grains, and nuts.

★ Drink at least 8 glasses of water.

BREAKFAST
Papaya & Spinach Soup (500ml/16fl oz)

SNACK
Fennel & Courgette Soup (500ml/16fl oz)

LUNCH
French Lentil Soup (500ml/16fl oz)

SNACK
Grapefruit & Fennel Soup (500ml/16fl oz)

DINNER
Butternut Black Bean Soup (500ml/16fl oz)

DESSERT
Raspberry Coconut Soup (250ml/9fl oz)

ALTERNATIVES
Mushroom & Millet Soup (dinner)
RECIPE PAGE 141

Beetroot & Orange Soup (snack)
RECIPE PAGE 40

★ Drink 2 glasses of alkalized water between meals.

★ Perform 30–60 minutes of light to moderate exercise daily during cleanse. Yoga in particular is very good for improving digestion.

★ You may choose to receive a colonic treatment halfway through or at the end of your cleanse if you find them helpful.

GINGER BEEF BONE BROTH

The longer you simmer this **rich, savoury** broth, the more **nutrients and minerals** are extracted from the bones. **Ginger** adds a spicy note, but it can be omited to make a **basic beef bone broth.** Serve hot.

PREP & COOK
10 to 48 hours

QUANTITY
Makes 2 litres (3½ pints)
Serving size 500ml (16fl oz)

STORAGE
Refrigerated 5 days
Frozen 8 weeks

INGREDIENTS

2kg (4lb) beef bones (neck, knucklebones, ribs, shank)

4 tbsp olive oil

3 litres (5¼ pints) water

2 tbsp apple cider vinegar

150g (5½oz) onion, diced

150g (5½oz) carrot, diced

100g (3½oz) celery, diced with leaves removed

8 garlic cloves, peeled

1 bay leaf

3 tbsp tomato purée

½ bunch parsley

4 tbsp fresh ginger, grated (optional)

NUTRITION PER SERVING

calories	64
total fat	0g
cholesterol	0mg
sodium	65mg
carbohydrate	14g
dietary fibre	3g
sugars	6g
protein	2g

METHOD

1 Preheat oven to 230°C (450°F/Gas 8) and line a baking tray with foil. In a large bowl, toss beef bones with olive oil to coat. Spread bones on prepared tray and roast for 20–30 minutes. (Roasting intensifies the flavour of the broth.)

2 Using tongs, carefully transfer bones to a large casserole. Add water, ensuring that water covers bones by at least 7.5–10cm (3–4 inches). Stir in apple cider vinegar. Cook over medium-high heat until water begins to the boil, about 35 minutes.

3 Reduce heat to simmer and cover. Continue to cook for a minimum of 9 hours or up to 48 hours. Intermittently skim broth to remove the impurities that rise to the top, and add water as needed to keep bones covered.

4 Two hours before removing the broth from the stove, add onion, carrot, celery, garlic, bay leaf, tomato purée, and parsley. Continue to simmer for 2 hours, and then remove pot from heat.

5 Strain broth, discarding vegetables and bones. Stir in fresh grated ginger (if using) and transfer to fridge to cool. Once cool, skim hardened fat from surface. Heat before serving and season with salt and pepper if needed.

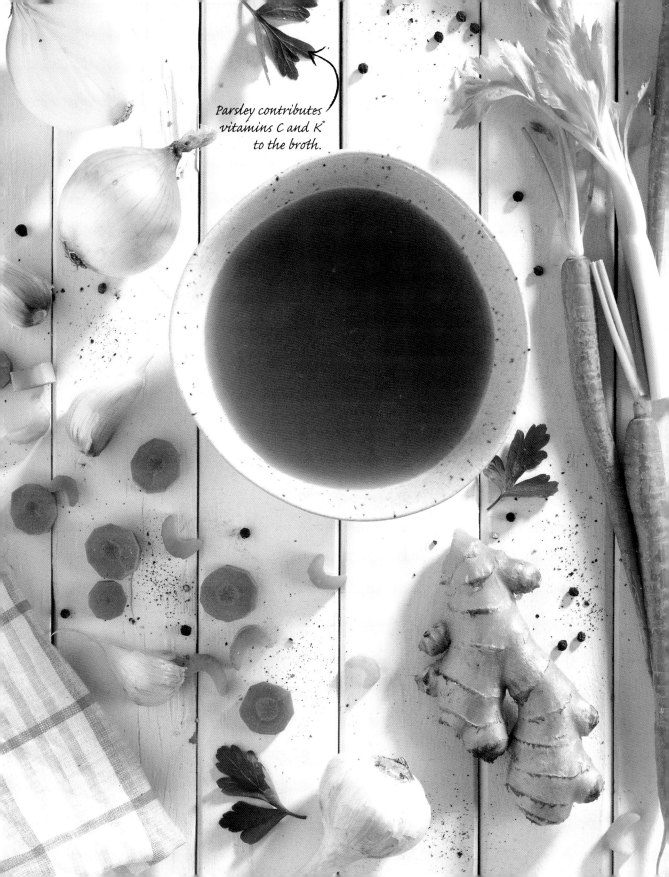

Parsley contributes vitamins C and K to the broth.

ROASTED VEGETABLE STOCK

Roasting vegetables causes them to caramelize, giving this stock **richness** and **depth of flavour**. It makes a **robust vegan base** for soups and stews, or enjoy on its own. Serve hot.

 **PREP & COOK**
1 hour 35 minutes

 QUANTITY
Makes 1.5 litres (2¾ pints)
Serving size 500ml (16fl oz)

 STORAGE
Refrigerated 5 days
Frozen 8 weeks

INGREDIENTS

115g (4oz) carrot, chopped
175g (6oz) leek, chopped
75g (2½oz) celery, chopped
35g (1¼oz) field
    mushroom, chopped
8 garlic cloves, peeled
2 tbsp olive oil
2 tbsp tomato purée
2 litres (3½ pints) water
5 stalks parsley
3 stalks thyme
1 tsp black peppercorns
1 bay leaf
¼ tsp salt
¼ tsp pepper

METHOD

1 Preheat oven to 220°C (425°F/Gas 7). In a roasting tin, combine carrots, leeks, celery, and garlic. Drizzle with olive oil and toss to coat. Roast vegetables for 20 minutes, or until they begin to brown.

2 Remove vegetables from tin and set aside. Place roasting tin on hob across two burners set to medium heat. Add 250ml (9fl oz) water and deglaze pan by running a wooden spoon around the bottom to remove browned vegetables.

3 Transfer liquid to casserole and add remaining water, roasted vegetables, tomato purée, parsley, thyme, peppercorns, and bay leaf. Bring to the boil over high heat and then reduce heat, cover, and simmer for 45 minutes.

4 Strain stock and discard vegetables. Skim off any remaining fat and season with salt and pepper.

NUTRITION PER SERVING

calories	27	carbohydrate	3g
total fat	1g	dietary fibre	1g
cholesterol	0mg	sugars	2g
sodium	203mg	protein	1g

BEEF & POULTRY BONE BROTH

The **mixture of meat bones** brings **layers of flavour**, complexity, and body to this broth. **Rejuvenating and restorative**, it is excellent on its own or as a **base for other soups**. Serve hot.

 PREP & COOK
10 to 36 hours

 QUANTITY
Makes 2 litres (3½ pints)
Serving size 500ml (16fl oz)

 STORAGE
Refrigerated 5 days
Frozen 8 weeks

INGREDIENTS

4 tbsp olive oil
680g (1½lb) beef bones (neck, knucklebones, ribs, shank)
680g (1½lb) turkey bones (neck, back)
680g (1½lb) chicken bones (neck, back, feet)
3 litres (5¼ pints) water
2 tbsp apple cider vinegar
150g (5½oz) onion, chopped
150g (5½oz) carrot, chopped
100g (3½oz) celery, chopped
8 garlic cloves, whole
1 bay leaf
3 tbsp tomato purée
½ bunch parsley
½ tsp salt
¼ tsp pepper

METHOD

1 Preheat oven to 200°C (400°F/Gas 6). Line a baking tray with foil. Toss bones with olive oil to coat. Spread bones on prepared tray and roast for 20–30 minutes.

2 Using tongs, carefully transfer bones to a large casserole. Add water, ensuring that water covers bones by at least 7.5–10cm (3–4 inches). Stir in apple cider vinegar. Cook over medium-high heat until water boils, about 35 minutes.

3 Reduce heat to simmer and cover. Continue to cook for a minimum of 9 hours or up to 36 hours. Intermittently skim broth, and add water as needed to keep bones covered.

4 Two hours before removing the broth from the hob, add onion, carrot, celery, garlic, bay leaf, tomato purée, and parsley. Continue to simmer for 2 hours.

5 Strain broth, discarding vegetables and bones. Season with salt and pepper to taste.

NUTRITION PER SERVING

calories	14	carbohydrate	3g
total fat	0g	dietary fibre	1g
cholesterol	0mg	sugars	2g
sodium	306mg	protein	1g

TAMARI & LEMON BROTH

This **light, cleansing broth** is restorative and hydrating. Rich in **vitamins and minerals,** it has **savoury depth** from tamari and a **light tanginess** from lemon. Serve hot.

PREP & COOK
1 hour 20 minutes

QUANTITY
Makes 1 litre (1¾ pints)
Serving size 500ml (16fl oz)

STORAGE
Refrigerated 5 days
Frozen 8 weeks

INGREDIENTS

1 tbsp olive oil

150g (5½oz) onion, chopped

150g (5½oz) carrot, chopped, plus 75g (2½oz) carrot, sliced into thin strips

100g (3½oz) celery, chopped

3 garlic cloves

30g (1oz) fresh parsley, chopped

1 bay leaf

1.5 litres (2¾ pints) water

120ml (4fl oz) lemon juice (about 5 lemons)

2 tbsp tamari

50g (1¾oz) mushrooms, chopped

85g (3oz) baby spinach

METHOD

1 In a medium casserole, heat olive oil over medium heat for 2 minutes. Add onion, 150g (5½oz) chopped carrot, and celery. Cook until vegetables begin to soften, about 5 minutes.

2 Add water to pot, increase heat, and bring to the boil. Add garlic, fresh parsley, and bay leaf and reduce heat. Cover and simmer for 45 minutes. Remove from heat.

3 Strain broth and discard vegetable solids. Stir in lemon juice, tamari, remaining 75g (2½oz) sliced carrots, mushrooms, and spinach. Cover for 10 minutes to allow vegetables to soften in the hot broth.

NUTRITION PER SERVING

calories	150
total fat	4g
cholesterol	0mg
sodium	1,102mg
carbohydrate	28g
dietary fibre	6g
sugars	10g
protein	6g

TURMERIC CORIANDER BROTH

Home-made bone broth is the basis for this **healing tonic** that features **vibrantly hued turmeric**, which is known for its anti-inflammatory effects and **mood-boosting attributes.** Serve hot.

 PREP & COOK
40 minutes

 QUANTITY
Makes 2 litres (3½ pints)
Serving size 500ml (16fl oz)

 STORAGE
Refrigerated 5 days
Frozen 8 weeks

INGREDIENTS

1½ tbsp olive oil

50g (1¾oz) celery, chopped

75g (2½oz) carrot, chopped

35g (1¼oz) fresh ginger, chopped

8 garlic cloves, peeled

2 litres (3½ pints) Beef & Poultry Bone Broth

1 (5cm/2-inch) piece turmeric, grated

2 tbsp tamari

2 tsp coriander seeds

METHOD

1 In a large casserole, heat olive oil over medium heat for 2 minutes. Add celery, carrot, ginger, and garlic, and cook for 5 minutes.

2 Add Beef & Poultry Bone Broth (page 169), turmeric, tamari, and coriander to pot. Increase heat and bring to a boil, and then reduce heat, cover, and simmer for 20 minutes. Remove from heat.

3 Using a mesh seive or colander lined with muslin, strain broth, discarding vegetable solids.

NUTRITION PER SERVING

calories	84
total fat	2g
cholesterol	10mg
sodium	618mg
carbohydrate	11g
dietary fibre	2g
sugars	4g
protein	5g

To make...
a vegetarian or vegan version, use Shiitake Ginger Broth instead of bone broth.

TOMATO BROTH WITH DILL

Bright fennel brings out the **natural sweetness of tomatoes** in this delicate broth, while **citrusy dill** adds an aromatic finish. Red pepper flakes provide **mild heat** as well as a **metabolic boost.** Serve hot.

PREP & COOK
1 hour 10 minutes

QUANTITY
Makes 2 litres (3½ pints)
Serving size 500ml (16fl oz)

STORAGE
Refrigerated 5 days
Frozen 8 weeks

INGREDIENTS

2 tbsp olive oil

50g (1¾oz) onion, diced

30g (1oz) celery, diced

50g (1¾oz) carrot, peeled and diced

1 cup fennel, bulb and fronds, diced

1 tbsp garlic, crushed (about 3 cloves)

400g (14oz) chargrilled tomatoes, skins removed, seeded and chopped

½ tsp red pepper flakes

2 litres (3½ pints) water

½ tsp salt

¼ tsp pepper

3 tbsp fresh dill, finely chopped

METHOD

1 In a large casserole, heat 1 tablespoon olive oil over medium heat for 2 minutes. Add onion, celery, carrot, fennel, and garlic. Cook until onion is translucent, about 5 minutes. Add tomatoes and red pepper flakes, and cook for 5 minutes.

2 Add water, increase heat, and bring to the boil. Then reduce heat, cover, and simmer for 40 minutes.

3 In batches, transfer contents of pot to a blender and purée until smooth. Strain puréed soup through a fine mesh sieve and discard pulp.

4 Season with salt and pepper to taste. Finish with fresh dill and drizzle with remaining 1 tablespoon olive oil.

NUTRITION PER SERVING

calories	107	carbohydrate	10g
total fat	7g	dietary fibre	3g
cholestoral	0g	sugars	5g
sodium	561g	protein	2g

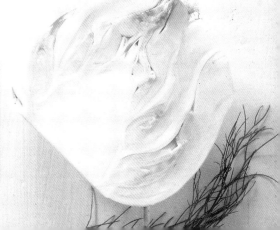

CHICKEN HERB CONSOMMÉ

Humble chicken soup is elevated with **classic French techniques,** yielding a **delicate consommé** with surprising depth of flavour, finished with a **sprinkling of fresh herbs.** Serve hot.

 **PREP & COOK**
1 hour 40 minutes

 QUANTITY
Makes 1.5 litres (2¾ pints)
Serving size 500ml (16fl oz)

 STORAGE
Refrigerated 5 days
Frozen 8 weeks

INGREDIENTS

2 stalks thyme, plus 1 tsp thyme, finely chopped

2 stalks parsley

1 bay leaf

½ tsp peppercorns

5 egg whites, chilled

50g (1¾oz) celery, diced

150g (5½oz) carrot, diced

150g (5½oz) onion, diced

450g (1lb) ground chicken, very chilled

2 litres (3½ pints) homemade chicken bone broth, chilled

1 tbsp chives, thinly sliced

½ tsp fresh rosemary

NUTRITION PER SERVING

calories	75
total fat	18g
cholesterol	175mg
sodium	625mg
carbohydrate	13g
dietary fibre	2g
sugars	8g
protein	47g

METHOD

1 Assemble aromatic sachet by placing thyme stalks, parsley stalks, bay leaf, and peppercorns in a muslin sachet bag.

2 In a small bowl, lightly beat egg whites until slightly frothy.

3 In a large casserole, combine beaten egg whites, celery, carrot, onion, ground chicken, chicken bone broth (page 156), and aromatic sachet. Bring to a simmer over medium-high heat, stirring occasionally. Within about 25 minutes, a raft of foam should form on the surface.

4 Reduce heat so liquid is barely simmering. With a spoon, gently break a hole in the middle of the raft to allow the consommé to bubble through. Baste the raft with liquid from the centre, without breaking it, about every 15 minutes.

5 Simmer until broth is clear and flavour fully develops, about 1 hour. Remove from heat. Line a mesh sieve with muslin or a coffee filter, and place over a large bowl or pot. Carefully ladle broth from hole in raft into sieve.

6 Strained broth should be clear and free of impurities. Top with chives, rosemary, and remaining chopped thyme.

ANTI-INFLAMMATORY
3-DAY CLEANSE

Chronic inflammation has a domino effect that can undermine your overall health. It is directly linked to your diet, and poor choices such as foods high in sugar, saturated fats, trans fats, refined carbohydrates, MSG, and aspartame can cause inflammation to worsen. Use this cleanse to help combat inflammation in the body and for restorative purposes.

Follow for 3 days. Afterwards, use as a 1-day cleanse on a weekly basis or incorporate individual soups into your daily diet.

shopping List

Fridge/Freezer
Kale (60g/2oz, chopped)
Baby spinach (85g/3oz)
Onions (4)
Red onion (1)
Carrots (7)
Celery (10 stalks)
Red pepper (2)
Yellow pepper (2)
Orange pepper (2)
Cucumber (1)
Beetroots (3 large)
Garlic (23 cloves)
Fennel (2 bulbs)
Fresh ginger (7.5cm/3-inch piece)
Kiwis (4)
Braeburn apples (6)
Limes (9)
Green grapes (175g/6oz, halved)
Mint (6 tsp, minced)
Parsley (1 bunch)
Beef bones (1.5kg/3 lb)
Turkey bones (1.5kg/3 lb)
Chicken bones (1.5kg/3 lb)

Pantry
Olive oil (250ml/9fl oz)
Apple cider vinegar (4 tbsp)
Red wine vinegar (3 tbsp)
Purified water (10 litres/17½ pints)
Agave nectar (4 tsp)
Amaranth (400g/14oz, cooked)
Freekeh (150g/5½oz, cooked)
Quinoa (125g/4½oz) cooked)
Tomato purée (6 tbsp)
Chopped tomatoes (6 x 400g cans)
Tomato juice (750ml/1¼ pints)
Coconut water (1.7 litres/3 pints)
Cinnamon sticks (6)
Bay leaves (2)
Salt
Pepper

PREPARATION

1 WEEK BEFORE

★ Make **Beef & Poultry Bone Broth** (double 500ml/16fl oz portions.
RECIPE PAGE 169

★ Make **Ancient Grains Soup** (triple batch); freeze in 500ml/16fl oz portions.
RECIPE PAGE 134

★ Eliminate processed foods and sugar from your diet and focus on whole foods.

2 DAYS BEFORE

★ Make **Kiwi Kale Gazpacho** (double batch); refrigerate in 250ml/9fl oz portions.
RECIPE PAGE 36

★ Make **Apple & Amaranth Soup** (double batch); refrigerate in 500ml/16fl oz portions.
RECIPE PAGE 100

★ Eliminate poultry, meat, and dairy from your diet.

★ Focus on vegetable-based meals supplemented with fish, grains, and legumes.

1 DAY BEFORE

★ Make **Beetroot Soup with Fennel** (triple batch); refrigerate in 500ml/16fl oz portions.
RECIPE PAGE 58

★ Make **Mixed Pepper Gazpacho** (triple batch); refrigerate in 500ml/16fl oz portions.
RECIPE PAGE 85

★ Transfer Beef & Poultry Bone Broth and Ancient Grains Soup from freezer to fridge to thaw.

★ Eliminate all animal products from your diet.

★ Eat vegetable-based meals with some legumes, grains, and nuts.

★ Drink at least 8 glasses of water.

DURING THE CLEANSE

DAILY SOUPS

BREAKFAST
Apple & Amaranth Soup (500ml/16fl oz)

SNACK
Beef & Poultry Bone Broth (500ml/16fl oz)

LUNCH
Mixed Pepper Gazpacho (500ml/16fl oz)

SNACK
Beetroot Soup with Fennel (500ml/16fl oz)

DINNER
Ancient Grains Soup (500ml/16fl oz)

DESSERT
Kiwi Kale Gazpacho (250ml/9fl oz)

ALTERNATIVES
Ginger Sweet Potato Soup (snack)
RECIPE PAGE 96

Strawberry Rhubarb Soup (dessert)
RECIPE PAGE 54

CLEANSE BOOSTERS

★ Drink 2 glasses of alkalized water between meals.

★ Perform 30–60 minutes of light to moderate exercise daily during cleanse, particularly Pilates or yoga.

The mix of onion,
carrot, and celery
that traditionally
forms the base of
many soups is
called mirepoix.

VEGETABLE BROTH WITH BASIL

This **refreshing, light, and lemony** broth is the **perfect remedy** for the cold season. For a **versatile vegetable soup base**, freeze a portion after straining and omit the **lemon and basil.** Serve hot.

PREP & COOK
1 hour

QUANTITY
Makes 2 litres (3½ pints)
Serving size 500ml (16fl oz)

STORAGE
Refrigerated 5 days
Frozen 8 weeks

INGREDIENTS

1 tbsp olive oil

300g (10oz) onion, diced

100g (3½oz) celery, diced

150g (5½oz) carrot, peeled and diced

8 garlic cloves, whole

6 stalks parsley

2 litres (3½ pints) water

1 bay leaf

1 tbsp black peppercorns, whole

Juice of 4 lemons

½ tsp salt

¼ tsp pepper

½ cup fresh basil, finely chopped

METHOD

1 In a large casserole, heat olive oil over medium heat for 2 minutes. Add onion, celery, carrot, and garlic. Cook until onion is translucent, about 5 minutes.

2 Add water, parsley, bay leaf, and peppercorns. Increase heat and bring to the boil, and then reduce heat, cover, and simmer for 40 minutes. Remove from heat.

3 Strain broth and discard vegetable solids. Stir in lemon juice and season with salt and pepper to taste. Leave to cool slightly before adding basil to prevent discolouration.

For an added...
metabolism boost, add very thinly sliced jalapeño or serrano pepper to broth.

NUTRITION PER SERVING	
calories	17
total fat	0g
cholesterol	0mg
sodium	293mg
carbohydrate	6g
dietary fibre	1g
sugars	1g
protein	1g

CHILLED TOMATO CONSOMMÉ

This **light, chilled soup** captures the **essence of summer tomatoes**, highlighted with the **fresh herbal notes** of basil, tarragon, and chives. Enjoy as a **refreshing afternoon meal** or snack. Serve chilled.

 PREP & COOK
4 hours

 QUANTITY
Makes 1.5 litres (2¾ pints)
Serving size 500ml (16fl oz)

 STORAGE
Refrigerated 4 days
Frozen 8 weeks

INGREDIENTS

1kg (2¼lb) ripe tomatoes, quartered and cored

2 cups fennel, bulb and fronds, finely chopped

2 garlic cloves, whole

300g (10oz) onion, diced

2 tsp sherry vinegar

2 tbsp olive oil

2 tbsp fresh basil, finely chopped

1 tbsp fresh tarragon, finely chopped

1 tbsp chives, thinly sliced

¼ tsp salt

METHOD

1 In a blender or food processor, combine tomatoes, fennel, garlic, and onion. Purée until smooth.

2 Line a large, non-reactive bowl with a double layer of muslin. Pour puréed vegetable mixture into the muslin, and then bring all four corners together and tie them to a wooden spoon. Place the spoon across the bowl so that the muslin is hanging and contents can drip into bowl.

3 Transfer bowl with hanging muslin to fridge and leave to sit for 4–6 hours, or until the majority of the liquid has dripped through (it should yield about 1.5 litres/2¾ pints). Discard muslin and pulp.

4 Before serving, stir in sherry vinegar, olive oil, basil, tarragon, chives, and salt.

NUTRITION PER SERVING

calories	216
total fat	10g
cholesterol	0mg
sodium	248mg
carbohydrate	30g
dietary fibre	8g
sugars	16g
protein	6g

Experiment with...
different herbs or even citrus flavours. Try dill and chive, or coriander and lime zest.

For the greatest
yield, use juicy
tomato varieties
with a high pulp
content.

VUELVE A LA VIDA BROTH

Come back to life with this **spicy and restorative broth.** Warm, earthy cumin **boosts immunity** and **aids digestion,** while ground chillies clear congestion and **improve metabolism.** Serve hot.

 **PREP & COOK**
1 hour 10 minutes

 QUANTITY
Makes 2 litres (3½ pints)
Serving size 500ml (16fl oz)

 STORAGE
Refrigerated 5 days
Frozen 8 weeks

INGREDIENTS

1 tbsp olive oil

225g (8oz) onion, diced

150g (5½oz) carrot, peeled and diced

100g (3½oz) celery, diced

8 garlic cloves, whole

4 tbsp tomato purée

2 litres (3½ pints) water

5 stalks parsley

1½ tsp ancho chilli powder

1 tbsp ground cumin

¾–½ tsp chile de árbol or cayenne powder

¼ tsp salt

Juice of 4 limes

4 tbsp coriander, finely chopped

METHOD

1 In a large casserole, heat olive oil over medium heat for 2 minutes. Add onion, carrot, celery, and garlic. Cook until onion is translucent, about 5 minutes. Add tomato purée and cook for another 5 minutes.

2 Add water and parsley to pot. Increase heat and bring to a boil, and then reduce heat to simmer. Add ancho chilli powder, cumin, and chile de árbol (adjust amount as desired). Cover and simmer for 40 minutes.

3 With a mesh sieve or colander lined with muslin, strain the broth, discarding vegetable solids. Season with salt and lime juice. Garnish with coriander just before serving.

To make...
Tortilla Soup, add 225g (8oz) chargrilled tomatoes, skinned and chopped, 125g (4½oz) black beans, 1 sliced avocado, and a handful of crumbled tortilla chips.

NUTRITION PER SERVING

calories	38
total fat	2g
cholesterol	0mg
sodium	88mg
carbohydrate	6g
dietary fibre	1g
sugars	2g
protein	2g

Red chilli peppers reduce cholesterol and improve overall heart health.

Sweetcorn is at its best at the end of summer. Make large batches of this broth and freeze to enjoy months later.

SWEETCORN BROTH

This **sweet and flavourful vegan broth** is perfect on its own or as a base for preparing **soups and cooked grains.** The broth is not only **mineral rich,** but also provides **vitamin C and folic acid.** Serve hot.

PREP & COOK
1 hour 10 minutes

QUANTITY
Makes 1.5 litres (2¾ pints)
Serving size 500ml (16fl oz)

STORAGE
Refrigerated 5 days
Frozen 8 weeks

INGREDIENTS

1 tbsp coconut oil
50g (1¾oz) celery, diced
75g (2½oz) onion, diced
6 ears sweetcorn, kernels removed and cobs reserved
2 stalks fresh thyme
2 stalks fresh parsley
1 bay leaf
1 tsp black peppercorns
2 litres (3½ pints) water
¼ tsp salt

METHOD

1 In a large casserole, heat coconut oil over medium heat for 2 minutes. Add celery and onion and cook until vegetables are translucent, about 5 minutes.

2 Add sweetcorn kernels, corn cobs, thyme, parsley, bay leaf, black peppercorns, and water. Increase heat and bring to the boil, and then reduce heat, cover, and simmer for 40 minutes.

3 Strain to remove vegetable solids, leaving just the broth behind. Season with salt to taste.

Set aside...
100g (3½oz) of sweetcorn kernels and purée with the broth for increased dietary fibre and a thicker texture.

NUTRITION PER SERVING

calories	16
total fat	1g
cholesterol	0mg
sodium	99mg
carbohydrate	1g
dietary fibre	0g
sugars	0g
protein	0g

INDEX

ABOUT THE AUTHOR

Alison Velázquez is a wellness professional and founder of Soupology, a company specializing in innovative, health-focused soups. Soupology has been featured on the TODAY Show and is at the forefront of the new souping trend. With a background in both fitness and culinary arts, Alison has passion for healthy living that spans across all aspects of her life. A graduate of the School of Business at the University of Illinois, Alison also received a certification in Pilates in 2009 and a Culinary Arts degree from Kendall College in Chicago. Having worked as both a private chef and caterer, she specializes in wellness cooking, utilizing fresh, seasonal ingredients to create light, unique fare. A vegetarian for nearly 20 years, Alison's specialty also lies in restricted dietary approaches, including vegan, Paleo, low carb, and gluten free.

AUTHOR'S ACKNOWLEDGMENTS

Credit is due to so many amazing supportive people who have helped shape and produce this unique cookbook.

Thanks to my family for teaching me the value of fresh quality ingredients, a deep appreciation for great food, and the value of a day's hard work.

To all of my friends and to Bug, thank you for your unwavering enthusiastic support; it's made all the difference.

A huge thank you to my clients for always supporting each of my new ventures and for having a genuine interest and commitment to healthy living that keeps me motivated and inspired to keep creating!

To all my Pilates people. You've been my reason to get out of bed every morning. Literally. Lucky for me, your commitment to your health and the latest gossip has been unwavering.

Thanks to Brook Farling, Ann Barton, and all those at DK who took a chance on me and made this whole project possible.

Thank you to Nigel Wright, Brian Wetzstein, and Mollie Hayward, who brought my recipes to life through their beautiful photos and styling.

And a special thanks to Kimberley Watry for her wisdom and always lending an ear and a glass of wine for my countless quandaries.

PUBLISHER'S ACKNOWLEDGMENTS

The publisher would like to thank Maxine Pedliham – her trendspotting led to the publication of this book. Thanks are also due to Mary Rodavich, MS, RD, LDN for providing the nutritional analysis and to Carolyn Doyle for testing the recipes.